NUTRITIONSTRIPPED

NUTRITION
STRIPPED

WHOLE-FOOD RECIPES MADE DELICIOUSLY SIMPLE

McKel Hill, MS, RDN

WM
WILLIAM MORROW
*An Imprint of HarperCollins*Publishers

This book is written as a source of information only. The information contained in this book should by no means be considered a substitute for the advice of a qualified medical professional, who should always be consulted before beginning any new diet, exercise, or other health program.

All efforts have been made to ensure the accuracy of the information contained in this book as of the date published. The author, publisher, and contributors expressly disclaim responsibility for any adverse effects arising from the use or application of the information contained herein.

HarperCollins books may be purchased for educational, business, or sales promotional use. For information please e-mail the Special Markets Department at SPsales@harpercollins.com.

FIRST EDITION

Designed by Ashley Tucker
Food photography by Katie Newburn
Portrait photography by Kelsey Cherry or Crystal Martel
Food styling and creative direction by McKel Hill

Library of Congress Cataloging-in-Publication Data has been applied for.

ISBN 978-0-06-241992-7

16 17 18 19 20 OV/QGT 10 9 8 7 6 5 4 3 2 1

I DEDICATE THIS BOOK TO YOU.
You're part of a global movement and shift to nourishing our bodies in the way nature intended, simple and back to bare basics. I hope this cookbook guides you to live better, inspires you to create in your kitchen, and infuses as much nourishment into your bodies as it does inspiration for your mind and happiness in your heart. This is just the beginning.

Thank you from the bottom of my heart for sharing this space with me; to you I will be forever thankful and inspired to create!

For Mom, Dad, and Josh, with all my love and light.

x M

CONTENTS

INTRODUCTION

*Health is a state of complete physical, mental and social well-being,
and not merely the absence of disease or infirmity.*
—WORLD HEALTH ORGANIZATION

The part can never be well unless the whole is well.
—PLATO

My philosophy about living whole and eating well extends far beyond that of eating or dieting and has everything to do with the entire framework of your lifestyle and well-being. It's about cultivating balance, happiness, and inner strength; managing stress; nourishing relationships; engaging in supportive communities; and taking care of your physical body as well as your mental, emotional, spiritual body. We must, *we must,* start taking better care of ourselves and respecting our bodies and the vast potential that's within us. Nourishing your cells with fuel from beautiful whole food is the catalyst.

Growing up, I knew food was good for us and loved eating, but beyond that I never realized the power that nutrition had on the way we felt. Until I had to. It wasn't until I started experiencing horrible migraines in high school that traveled with me into college that I knew my lifestyle had an impact on the way I felt. Initially I went to a neurologist and began taking prescription medications, but although I no longer *felt* the migraine, I didn't feel anything else either. The lethargy took me out of my element. I had trouble doing the things I normally enjoyed—like creating art and hanging out with friends. I'm talking about your basic functions of being human! For years, this was my life, kind of just "dealing" with this on and off because there was no other solution. Fast-forward a couple of college majors later, and I landed at my home base. The world of nutrition.

In high school and the early years of college, I used to consume "health" foods that weren't the best for my body, mind, or spirit—they were heavily processed quick fixes, full of ingredients I could barely pronounce. These foods never made me feel well physically or look my best either; instead I had poor digestion, low energy during workouts, and dull skin and hair. I wasn't feeling good, radiant, or balanced. I knew something had to give.

Another fast-forward to honing in on my research, studies, and academic experience, I found what worked for me and what didn't. Using protocol and nutrition phases as I do now with my clients, I noticed a radical shift in my health within weeks of replacing foods I was sensitive to (dairy and gluten) and changing my lifestyle and healing my gut. I no longer felt bloated, my digestion issues resolved, my hair grew longer and stronger, my acne breakouts started to clear, *I had immense energy, my athletic performance increased, and, best of all, my migraine headaches decreased dramatically.* I know what it's like to feel unhealthy, subpar, and unbalanced—and I never want to look back. If I have the ability to help you find your inner health, whether you feel like it's buried in your core or just about to break the surface, then I'm here. I'm here because I want to help you. Nourishing your body with whole foods is the first step you can take to a healthier and happier life.

> I'm here because I want to help you. Nourishing your body with whole foods is the first step you can take to a healthier and happier life.

Our bodies are multidimensional, unique, and beautiful in their own ways—remember this the next time you read a blogger recommending a juice fast or a tabloid boasting about the latest diet trend a celebrity is following, or when a friend suggests that you eat *x* pounds of fruit a day or tells you that you can cure an illness overnight by eliminating everything "toxic." It's all too dogmatic and impractical, and quite frankly, it's missing the biggest piece of the puzzle that is *your* uniqueness. We're all incredibly different, and when it comes to nourishing your body, transforming your health, or finding your healthy and happy weight, it all depends on *you*. The only way you can ever find the magic sweet spot is adjusting your lifestyle so that it works for you, not against you, and helps reap the benefits you desire. My approach to healthful living is simple: going back to bare basics and stripping away all the confusion, the past ideals, societal pressures, and giving you the tools *to do YOU* . . . which is infinitely more amazing than you may think.

The recipes in this book are rooted in simplicity, but they also incorporate a little fun with a global fusion of flavors. You may see ingredients that are new to you and your kitchen. When cooking with global flavors I do my best to keep with that region's traditional ingredient, but often you'll see a play on a traditional dish that draws on ingredients from different regions: The Turmeric Aebleskivers with Mango Jam (page 131) combine Indian flavors with a traditional Danish recipe. Chocolate and cinnamon, traditional in Mexican cuisine, are introduced to an American classic in Chocolate-Cinnamon-Walnut Chili (page 161). And Indian spice is fused with an American barbecue staple in Corn on the Cob with Tamarind-Date Chutney (page 225). Since many of my recipes use seasonal ingredients, always consider your region and what season you're cooking in. For example, if a recipe calls for spring green peas and it's winter, consider using asparagus, broccoli, or squash. In a nutshell, be flexible and go with the ebb and flow of the seasons.

I use a variety of kitchen tools and equipment, but don't feel obligated to go shopping to pick up every single piece—I have a list of my tops on page 266. When I talk about blenders, I'm always referring to the high-speed kind; this is the class of blenders that will make your smoothies ridiculously smooth and will have enough power to make nut/seed butters. I even opt for a blender instead of a whisk or food processor when combining batters and doughs for ease of cleanup!

The Nutrition Stripped way of living encompasses more than just food and nutrition. Other pillars of this "whole" lifestyle that keep you living well include stress management, exercise, cultivating healthful and positive relationships with others, sleeping well, drinking water, attending to spiritual health, and engaging in work that makes you truly happy!

THE
NUTRITION
STRIPPED WAY

Whole foods. Whole living. Plant-centric.
Nourishing. Optimizing. Simple. Delicious!
As a dietitian nutritionist, I will show you
how to strip away nutrition confusion
layer by layer and get back to the
bare basics of whole, nourishing foods
and what it means to live well.

FOOD PHILOSOPHY

*It's difficult to think anything but pleasant thoughts
while eating a homegrown tomato.*
—LEWIS GRIZZARD

I want to show you that eating nutritious foods and living a whole lifestyle can transform your well-being on all levels, nourishing your body from inside your cells so it radiates out. That's some powerful stuff! I know what it feels like to be out of balance and miss lightness and pep in your step, but if I can manifest a healthful life, I know you can too. Plus, I did a lot of the hard work of figuring out tips and tricks so you don't have to. The Nutrition Stripped food philosophy is rooted in these core nutrition principles:

1. GET BACK TO BASICS. Be a hunter, forager, and gatherer in the twenty-first century! Support local food, farmers, and artisans. As much as possible, eat foods that are organic. Opt for real whole foods that you can trace back to the source.

2. CONSUME MORE PLANTS. Scientific research has clearly shown the many health benefits of eating a diet high in plant foods from the earth: fruits, vegetables, nuts, seeds, grains, pseudo-grains (including gluten-free grains like quinoa and buckwheat), legumes, and beans. We don't need science to tell us how good eating plants makes us feel—try it for yourself and befriend these powerhouses of nutrition!

3. **KNOW YOUR FARMER.** If you consume animal proteins in your diet, make sure they have been humanely raised and have been fed their natural diets. You should be able to trace your food back to the source and know where the animal was raised and fed, and how it existed (e.g., grass fed, wild caught, pasture raised, free range, organic). The well-being of animals we consume matters. As Michael Pollan said best, "You are what you eat eats."

4. **WATCH FOR THE REAL DEAL.** If you read a food ingredient listed on a package that you wouldn't be able to find in your grandma's pantry, just walk away and look for the real deal. Cook from home more often to re-create those premade foods yourself; they'll taste much better. Better yet, eat foods without a food label and make a meal in your own kitchen from scratch.

5. **PRACTICE MINDFULNESS.** Nutrition isn't all about counting calories, grams of fat, and fiber, nor is eating only for the purpose of sustenance. Food plays many roles in the social, mental, emotional, cultural, and physical aspects of our lives. We should respect those roles. We all, myself included, need to spend a little more time enjoying food and "freeing" our brains from the mathematics of food, diet fads, and nutritional dogmas.

6. **BE FLEXIBLE.** Granted, as much as we all would love to follow a program to a T with no mess-ups, guess what? This is not a diet. I repeat, this is not a diet! It's a lifestyle, and life is full of external circumstances and changes; it ebbs and flows. We too need to respect and honor our ever-changing lifestyles and allow for some flexibility in what we eat and do. It's okay to dine out and indulge every now and then. As long as the majority of your food intake nourishes you, make a little room for dining out with zero guilt.

THE BALANCING PILLARS
OF LIVING WHOLE AND EATING WELL

*Eating food should be just as enjoyable to your taste buds
as it is nourishing to your cells.*
—YOURS TRULY

The easiest way to start taking care of yourself and finding what works for you is to draw attention to the following areas in your lifestyle and see where you can improve, what areas are stronger than others, and how you can make tweaks to find that sweet spot you've been searching for.

1. SLEEP. Yeah, yeah, we all know it. Sleeping is important, especially for regulating hunger and stress, which can tamper with the hormones that play a role in maintaining a healthful weight. Aim for seven to nine hours.
   Tip: Set your bedtime boundary and don't compromise those eight hours!

2. BE PRESENT. Meditation is the ultimate tool. Take the time to create mental space using meditation, which allows your mind to refocus, reenergize, cultivate happiness, and ultimately be more productive. For me, it's a daily practice I schedule in my morning routine and I immediately reap the benefits of feeling more connected.

   Tip: If you're a beginner, try guided meditations through audio or video guides and check out my favorite resources on page 289.

3. GET ORGANIZED. Finding organization in your life is helpful to managing your time and prioritizing your health, social life, career, and everything else that calls to us during the day. Try using productivity tools or apps that help you feel balanced, focused, and organized.

Tip: Start your day with a to-do list and prioritize those tasks that you *must* get done before anything else.

4. REALITY > SOCIAL MEDIA. I love social media—it's brought Nutrition Stripped places I never dreamed of. But let's face it, social media can be a huge distraction from what's real and truly important at the end of the day. One minute you're just checking Instagram, the next you're opening a tab to Facebook, and then you're reading tweets and pinning. The cycle is vicious. Set your boundaries and be intentional about the information you allow to soak into your mind and subconscious—surround yourself with positive, authentic, truthful, and inspiring content!

Tip: I give myself set hours to use social media and stick to them. As much as I *love* sharing, there has to be a balance.

5. ESTABLISH A MORNING ROUTINE. This is so important! It's one of the first goals I set with my clients. Create a morning routine that allows you to start your day as centered as possible, whether that's meditating, taking a walk outside, having your morning coffee or Turmeric Milk (page 69), or reading. Too often we immediately start looking at social media and putting "junk" in our minds; start by doing activities that refuel you on all levels. It'll change the dynamic for your entire day.

Tip: Set your alarm earlier. Even if you're not a morning person, waking up fifteen to thirty minutes earlier can give you a bit more breathing room to clear your mind and start the day off on a good note.

6. EAT GREENS! Simple as that. Many of us fall shy of how many greens we should be eating per day; my recommendation is at least three servings of leafy greens in addition to other vegetables, up to eight servings a day. Try to consciously add more greens to your diet whenever you can. A simple way is to add greens to smoothies, stews, soups, salads, sandwiches, or juices.

Tip: The easiest way to instantly add more greens to your diet is by starting your morning off with my Stripped Green Smoothie (page 82), which has about four servings of vegetables per glass.

7. EAT BALANCED. Many of my female clients who have been on restrictive diets crave sugar and carbohydrates simply because they're not eating them at all, depriving

themselves of energy and not making up for it with proteins or healthful fats. Getting in a great balance of macronutrients throughout your day and week and ideally at each meal is vital to keep you feeling invincible.

Tip: Start with a plate or bowl full of greens or vegetables, and then add a protein (either from plants or a humanely raised animal), healthful fats, and a fiber-rich carbohydrate for balance.

8. MOVE AND SWEAT. My favorite forms of exercise are HIIT-style training, power walking, barre, restorative yoga, boxing, and so on; but moving your body is far more than working out consistently—it's also about moving throughout your day. Many of us have lost the element of routine walking and movement. Continual movement is good for our lymphatic system, which is stimulated by movement and is important for clearing the body of unwanted metabolites and waste as well as keeping our circulation healthy.

Tip: If you're sitting all day at work, make it a point to walk to the farthest restroom to take a break, walk outside for ten minutes, or even do a quick set of jumping jacks, wall squats, wall push-ups, or planks when you can.

9. LOVE. Whether it's going on a romantic date with your love, going out on the town with your friends, reading a book at your favorite coffee shop, making a phone date with home (Hi Mom!), hosting a girls' night, or keeping it low-key and hanging solo, you will nourish your health, heart, and overall well-being.

Tip: Find personal one-on-one time with a friend or loved one, and leave the phones behind. We often take for granted the power of human interaction and simple conversations.

10. ENJOY FRESH AIR AND NATURE. There's nothing better for your health than grounding to nature, breathing in fresh air, and feeling warm sunshine. Try taking a walk outside at a local park, hiking, gardening, playing with your dog, or riding a bike. Just get outside and enjoy the fresh air and sunshine (a.k.a. vitamin D!).

Tip: Make the time to spend at least thirty minutes outside every day. If you work indoors for long periods of time, set your alarm/calendar to go off every two hours to remind you to take a quick walk outside.

11. SPEND TIME WITH ANIMALS. Research has clearly shown that individuals with pets often experience greater happiness, connectedness, and well-being, which is why animals are used so often in rehabilitation programs, in therapy, and for service.

Tip: If bringing a pet into your family isn't possible, try volunteering at a local animal shelter or donating to your favorite animal charity. It'll make your heart happy and the animals will enjoy it as well.

12. CLEAR YOUR SPACE, CLEAR YOUR MIND. I operate off this motto especially because I work from home. If my studio space or home is a disaster, my mind is cluttered and completely distracted. Keeping a clear space also eases the flow between tasks and allows you to move with efficiency. On a spiritual level, I also view it as respect for your special and sacred place.

Tip: Take ten minutes before you start engaging in work to clean your space, tidy your desk, or clean house. Really, who can't spare ten minutes in order to better serve?

13. CHALLENGE YOURSELF. Be willing to do something that pushes you outside your comfort zone. I often make this a monthly goal and sometimes a daily goal, but either way I continually embrace those things that completely frighten me because it helps me grow. An example from my life: quitting all of my formal jobs to start my own business and . . . writing a cookbook! Both were completely terrifying, yet the best time of my life thus far.

Tip: At those uncomfortable moments, ask yourself, How can I challenge myself in this moment? Am I staying comfortable out of fear? Jump in and get started!

14. GIVE BACK. Giving back doesn't have to mean volunteering every week or month. It can take the form of extending common courtesies that some of us forget when we think we're too busy: opening a door for someone, picking up the tab for the person in line after you at the coffee shop, being kind to your neighbor, lending a hand to a friend who needs you, donating your time to a local shelter, and so on.

Tip: Sometimes all it takes is asking. Ask a friend or loved one if she needs help, and more often than not, she'll have something for you to do!

15. DO. What good are goals if we don't make any forward movements to accomplish them? Set goals, but also set them with the intention to complete them. Make goals that are not only realistic but also challenging.

Tip: Visualize your goal, how you feel living in that achievement, what it looks like, your lifestyle, surroundings, and so forth. Then write down your approach to solidify your vision, plan and prioritize, and take action!

16. GIVE GOOD ENERGY. I'm a big believer in the energy you put out in the world; your attitude, service, words, and actions can directly impact other areas of your life. A simple act of kindness or practicing gratitude and humility can be where it all starts.

Tip: Ever heard the saying "Check your energy at the door"? This is a simple mantra you can use to keep your positive and good energy in check. Sometimes our stress takes over, and before we know it, we've missed out on potentially amazing interactions because of our energy and distractions.

17. LOVE THYSELF. That's right. We can be brutal and critical when it comes to how we speak to ourselves. Loving yourself for who you are at your most authentic self is the first step in sharing your passions with the world and loving others. How would you speak to your six-year-old self? Do that!

Tip: Try out these positive mantras to keep your self-talk in a positive light: "I am beautiful." "I am confident." "I am strong." "I am healthy." "I am love." "I am joy."

18. MANAGE STRESS. Stress can have a deleterious effect on reaching your health goals. I know when I'm not taking the time to manage my stress and take breaks from work, because I begin to burn out, which then takes a toll on my body and mind. I can't *stress* this enough, but take the time and make it a priority every day to do something that helps you calm your mind.

Tip: To start out, schedule your stress-managing time as you would any other appointment: "meditation date with the meditation pillow at seven a.m. before work." Do something you freaking love first thing in the morning!

19. INDULGE IN ALONE TIME. It's human nature to socialize and to find comfort in community by bonding with other people, yet don't forget to take time just for you. You deserve it! It'll make it that much easier to keep your focus, energy, and body "fueled" and ready to give back to others when needed.

Tip: Whether it's taking a personal day off work to just read or go to the spa, or the simple act of "doing nothing" for thirty minutes a day, take some time for yourself to do whatever keeps you in your best form.

20. TRAVEL. Life's too short not to take notice of the other cultures in our world and completely dive in and live it! Even if you're unable to physically travel, it's nice to take time to research and learn about other cultures and the food, practices, and beauty in other parts of the world.

Tip: Have fun and make a travel to-do list. Even if travel isn't in your near future, you can still learn about other cultures by reading, watching documentaries, sifting through photography, or creating a Pinterest board to manifest your travel dreams! I have one that includes visiting Thailand, India, Copenhagen, Paris, Rome, Greece, Australia, London, New Zealand, Germany—and the list goes on!

KITCHEN ESSENTIALS

Stocking your pantry with nourishing foods is essential to eating well, which is the first step in optimizing your well-being. It's an amazing feeling to open up a pantry full of your favorite whole foods just waiting to be used in your next meal or snack, and it's great to be well stocked at all times just in case inspiration strikes to make a homemade nut butter, trail mix, truffles, soup, a batch of cookies, or anything else. Stocking your pantry and knowing what to include is truly the foundation of a healthful and happy kitchen. Ideally, I recommend purchasing produce from local markets and directly from farmers. Fresh, seasonal food is the most nutritious, but I understand not everyone has this access—even I don't in Nashville year-round. In that case, choose among the best options at the grocery store, and focus on organic and non-GMO foods. Otherwise, befriend your farmers and support local homegrown food.

TOP TEN GROCERY SHOPPING TIPS

1. Shop the perimeter of the store. This is where most fresh fruits and vegetables are found!

2. Shop farmers' markets and local farms for produce and proteins.

3. Shop wholesale retailers for discounted organic bulk items.

4. If purchasing something in a box, bag, or wrapper, be able to pronounce the names of the ingredients.

5. Buy in bulk for affordability and store in jars at home to keep products fresh.

6. Shop with reusable grocery bags.

7. Be a label detective, checking the ingredient list first instead of the numbers/nutrition label.

8. Avoid chemicals, artificial colorings, flavorings, and preservatives as much as possible.

9. Just because a package states "healthy," "natural," or "low fat" on the front of the box doesn't mean it's healthful. The ingredients list will always tell you the truth.

10. Aim to fill your grocery cart with 80 percent foods coming from the perimeter and 20 percent coming from the middle of the store (e.g., condiments, teas, spices, frozen foods).

WHEN PURCHASING . . .

Fruits and Vegetables

- Fresh is best!

- Frozen is next best. Choose frozen fruits and vegetables that contain no additives, such as sugar, spices, seasonings, and sauces, all of which can add unhealthful processed fats, sodium, and refined sugars.

- Choose organic when possible. Shop by using the Environmental Working Group's (EWG's) "Dirty Dozen" list as a guideline. (Go to www.ewg.org.)

- The nose knows! Gauge how ripe fruits and vegetables are by smelling and touching.

- Dark leafy greens should be crisp and sturdy in texture.

- Fruit shouldn't have wrinkled skin; it should feel heavy for its size.

REVIVING WILTED PRODUCE

Vegetables naturally lose moisture once they've been picked, especially after having been stored in the refrigerator. To help revive vegetables and make them crunchy and firm again, fill a large bowl with ice water, add the vegetables (slice to increase water absorption), and let soak for 15 minutes. Gently dry well before using or storing again.

Carbohydrates (Grains, Legumes, etc.)

- Choose whole-food carbohydrates (e.g., sweet potatoes, oatmeal, brown rice, quinoa).

- Choose high-fiber options when available (at least 3 to 4 grams fiber per serving).

- Choose products that have minimal ingredients.

- Avoid added sugar, high-fructose corn syrup, and trans fat.

- Be mindful of sodium content, always choosing no-salt-added or low- or reduced-sodium varieties.

- Avoid the "whites" (e.g., white bread, pasta, rice, crackers, tortillas). Opt instead for higher-fiber counterparts.

(continued on page 21)

DULSE STRIPS

HIJIKI

AGAR AGAR

KELP

DULSE FLAKES

NAKAME

COCOA POWDER

SPIRULINA

NUTRITIONAL YEAST

DRIED MULBERRIES

SHREDDED COCONUT

AÇAÍ POWDER

CACAO NIBS

GOJI BERRIES

MATCHA

CHLORELLA

MACA

ELDERBERRIES

BEE POLLEN

• Befriend gluten-free grains/carbohydrates (e.g., quinoa, millet, amaranth, oatmeal), which tend to be higher in protein and minerals.

Canned Foods and Frozen Products

• Check the sodium content. Choose no-added-salt or reduced-sodium varieties.

• Avoid canned vegetables and fruits with the exception of tomatoes and beans. Choose organic and cans that are free of bisphenol A (BPA).

• Seek out BPA-free cans overall.

• Be mindful of canned animal poteins. Search for organic and wild caught.

• Because frozen vegetables and fruits may contain added sugar, syrups, or flavorings, opt for brands that contain only said vegetable or fruit. For example, if you're buying frozen strawberries, the ingredients list should read "strawberries."

FREEZER ESSENTIALS

Bananas: Allow fresh bananas to get very ripe, then peel and place on a baking sheet in the freezer. Allow them to freeze completely (this keeps them from sticking together), remove from the baking sheet, and store in an airtight glass container. Use in smoothies, desserts, and more.

Other fruits: Strawberries, blueberries, tart cherries, blackberries, mulberries, mango, pineapple, young coconut meat, açaí, bananas, chopped apple, chopped pear.

Zucchini: Wash, chop, and freeze fresh zucchini in an airtight glass container. Use in smoothies, stews, soups, stir-fries, and more.

Other vegetables: Peas, corn, mixed vegetables, spinach, artichoke hearts, bell peppers, pearl onions, fava beans.

Grains: Artisan Seeded Bread (page 134), Raw Tart Shell (page 247).

GROCERY SHOPPING LIST

Growing your own produce is not only economical, it also provides the best guarantee of freshness. Many of us, of course, are not able to do that, so to make healthful eating afford-able, see "Twenty Ways to Eat Healthfully on a Budget" (page 24). Be sure to check yearly with the EWG about which foods should be purchased organic.

Fruit

- Lemons
- Oranges
- Grapefruits
- Tangerines
- Blueberries
- Strawberries
- Raspberries
- Blackberries
- Peaches
- Plums
- Nectarines
- Cherries
- Apricots
- Cantaloupes
- Watermelons
- Honeydew melons
- Mangoes
- Pineapples
- Papayas
- Guavas
- Kiwis
- Figs
- Dates
- Apples
- Pears
- Avocados
- Grapes
- Bananas

Vegetables

- Spinach
- Kale
- Romaine lettuce
- Arugula
- Belgian endives
- Watercress
- Baby mixed greens
- Mustard greens
- Collard greens
- Turnip greens

FROZEN

- Spinach
- Turnip greens
- Corn
- Any mixed vegetables such as carrots, broccoli, no seasonings/sauces
- Any mixed fruits or individual fruits, no added sauces or syrups

Protein Sources

ANIMAL

- Chicken, free-range, antibiotic-free
- Eggs, cage-free
- Beef, grass-fed
- Fish, including salmon, tilapia, and tuna, wild-caught and fresh if you live in coastal regions or flash-frozen (frozen at sea)
- Seafood, including shrimp and scallops, wild-caught and fresh if you live in coastal regions or flash-frozen (frozen at sea)

PLANT-BASED

- Tempeh
- Tofu, sprouted
- Beans (e.g., black, navy, lima, chickpeas, black-eyed peas, kidney)
- Lentils
- Split green peas
- Edamame
- Spirulina

Nondairy/Dairy

- Almond milk
- Coconut milk, canned organic, light
- Hemp seed milk
- Rice milk
- Oat milk
- Organic grass-fed butter or vegan butter
- Organic cheese, goat/ sheep milk
- Organic plain yogurt: coconut milk, rice milk, almond milk, goat milk

Condiments/Oils

- Mustard: Dijon, spicy, yellow
- Apple cider vinegar, raw
- Fermented veggies: kimchi, sauerkraut
- Oils: coconut oil, cold-pressed, extra-virgin olive oil, grapeseed oil
- Balsamic vinegar
- Hot sauce, low-sodium
- Nama shoyu (lower-sodium soy sauce)
- Soy sauce (low-sodium)
- Olives
- Honey, local
- Pure maple syrup
- Coconut aminos

Herbs/Spices (fresh or dried)

HERBS

- Basil
- Rosemary
- Thyme
- Mint
- Stevia
- Cilantro
- Parsley
- Dill
- Sage

SPICES

- Turmeric, curry powders
- Cinnamon
- Ginger
- Garlic
- Sea salt, black pepper
- Cayenne
- Red pepper flakes, chili powder
- Sumac

Grains

- Rice: brown, wild, basmati
- Oatmeal
- Quinoa
- Amaranth
- Buckwheat
- Millet
- Pasta: rice, quinoa, whole wheat
- Bread, high-fiber, gluten-free
- Crackers, high-fiber, gluten-free
- Soba noodles

Miscellaneous

- High-quality cocoa powder
- Cacao nibs
- Dark chocolate (80% cacao or higher)
- Goji berries, dried
- Spirulina/chlorella
- Bee pollen
- Coconut nectar
- Maca
- Shredded coconut, unsweetened
- Flours: almond, coconut, brown rice, peanut
- Stevia powder

PLANT-BASED PROTEIN

Regardless of whether you eat animal proteins, everyone can benefit from nutrient-dense plant-based protein and easily incorporate these into their diets on a daily or weekly basis. All nuts and seeds in the following chart are raw unless otherwise specified.

INGREDIENT	SERVING	PROTEIN
Lentils	1 cup cooked	18 g
Split green peas	1 cup cooked	16 g
Hemp seeds	3 tablespoons	~ 10 g
Chia seeds	3 tablespoons	6 g
Quinoa	1 cup cooked	~ 8 g
Spirulina	2 tablespoons	8 g
Nutritional yeast	2 tablespoons	18 g
Sunflower seeds	1 ounce	6 g
Sesame seeds	1 ounce	5 g
Flaxseeds	1 ounce	5 g
Pumpkin seeds	1 ounce	6 g
Almonds	1 ounce	6 g
Walnuts	1 ounce	7 g
Pistachios	1 ounce	6 g
Brazil nuts	1 ounce	4 g
Beans	1 cup	~ 15 g
Organic tempeh and tofu	4 ounces	20 g

TWENTY WAYS TO EAT HEALTHFULLY ON A BUDGET

1. BEFRIEND BEANS. Beans, lentils, legumes, pulses—whatever you may call them—are all fantastic ingredients to bulk up any meal in terms of volume, calories, and nutrition without costing you much. Dry pulses are great to purchase in bulk, and they store well in airtight glass containers or mason jars.

2. PRIORITIZE ORGANICS. Stick to the EWG's "Dirty Dozen" list for the top foods that should be purchased organic. This will help you cut down on the overall amount of organic produce you have to buy.

3. BULK UP. Buy in bulk as often as possible. At first, you may think you're spending a lot of money on bulk specialty items, but when you break down the cost per

serving, you're actually saving money in the long term. For example, I always buy spirulina, chia seeds, and hemp seeds in bulk. This can also be applied to your beans, grains, and other produce items.

4. SHOP SMART. Frequent wholesale stores and your local farmers' markets, buy a CSA (community-supported agriculture) share, or rent a plot at a community garden.

5. GARDEN. If you can't buy it, try to grow it! Gardens, whether personal or communal, are a great way to have local, seasonal, and healthful food right at your fingertips. It also is a great teaching/learning experience for everyone in the family.

6. SHOP ACCORDING TO THE SEASON. Remember the season! Trying to get strawberries in the dead of winter is quite expensive compared with purchasing them when they're perfectly ripe and local to your region in the summer.

7. EMBRACE FROZEN. Don't neglect the frozen aisle of your grocery stores (and no, I don't mean that you should stock up on highly processed frozen entrées). Look for frozen veggies and fruits with no added ingredients. If you're shopping for frozen raspberries, the only ingredient should be raspberries.

8. BATCH COOK! I've said it a million times, and I'll say it forever: Cooking in bulk or large batches will not only save you a tremendous amount of time for the week ahead, but it can also help you use all your bulk-purchased items to prepare meals for later by freezing. See page 269 for more inspiration!

9. SKIP THE "SUPERFOODS." "Superfoods," such as maca, goji berries, lucuma, spirulina, and medicinal mushrooms, are all the rage now, and I use them quite often, but all whole foods are "super" foods in my book!

10. LOVE NUTS AND SEEDS. Start cooking with nuts and seeds. Not only are they calorie dense but they're also nutrient dense for a very small amount. I often buy nuts and seeds in bulk not only because I'm constantly using them in recipes, but also because they're so easy to sprinkle onto salads, or use to make nut milks, desserts, and more.

11. STICK WITH HOMEMADE. Whenever possible, make your own version of the store-bought, including The Only Hummus You'll Ever Need (page 137), jams, soups, nut milk (see page 45) and nut butters (see page 43), ice creams, smoothies, juices, and so on. You're often paying

for the convenience and brand rather than the actual ingredients. Did I mention homemade foods are much healthier? Well, they are, and when you make your own food from scratch with quality ingredients that you've shopped for, you'll foster a connection with food that you otherwise wouldn't have when buying prepared foods.

12. **PREPARE YOUR OWN FROZEN MEALS.** Cooking large batches of beans and lentils, then freezing them in mason jars, can help you save time and stay within budget. Other ideas include cooking rice, roasted vegetables, or proteins of your choice and freezing them in glass containers.

13. **SHARE WITH FRIENDS.** Share the costs of healthful eating by buying in bulk or purchasing a CSA membership together.

14. **BE THE LAST ONE.** Purposefully try to catch the tail end of farmers' markets. Most often farmers are willing to negotiate a bit more because they'd rather sell their produce to someone than take it back home!

15. **MAKE A LIST.** Prioritize the foods and items you need by making a list before you leave the house. This helps cut down on impulse buys and keeps you on track with the meals you've planned!

16. **CLEAN OUT THE PANTRY.** It's smart to clear the house of foods and goods that don't necessarily mesh with your goals and lifestyle but can be donated. It's also a great way to take inventory of what you do have to prioritize for your next grocery trip.

17. **MAKE YOUR OWN JAMS AND SPECIAL CONDIMENTS.** Using frozen or leftover fresh fruit is a great way to make your own canned jams for several months ahead (see page 48). You're not wasting any fruit by discarding!

18. **BE SMART ABOUT STORAGE.** Storing your bulk items in airtight glass containers like mason jars helps to keep your grains, nuts, seeds, and beans optimally fresh. Arrange the items in your refrigerator in a way that ensures good air circulation. I find it useful to store all my greens in large BPA-free plastic bags or bins to keep them fresh rather than keeping them in store-bought packages or wrappers.

19. USE LEFTOVERS. Many of us end up with leftovers from cooking. Instead of wasting them or throwing them away, utilize the leftovers as ingredients in a quick stir-fry or salad bowl.

20. FLOUR POWER. Make your own flours! When you purchase grains, nuts, and seeds in bulk, you can process them in a high-speed blender or grinder to make your own flour. Store in a mason jar in the refrigerator for up to 2 weeks to keep it optimally fresh.

THE BASICS:
HOW TO . . .

Th==T==hese are essential skills everyone should have to live a whole-food lifestyle. Master them and make alterations as needed; they will form the foundation for your cooking going forward.

JUICE WITH A BLENDER

Many of us don't have a juicer or, in my case, sometimes I'm lazy and don't want to bring it out and clean up! Using your high-speed blender with cheesecloth may be your new favorite way to make a simple juice.

1. Blend together all the ingredients until smooth.

2. Line a pitcher with a nut-milk bag or cheesecloth.

3. Pour the blended mixture into the nut-milk bag, straining and squeezing with your hands.

4. Squeeze all the juice possible from the pulp.

5. Discard the pulp (or compost it).

Use It: Try this easy method to make Garden Pineapple (page 63) or Watermelon Herb (page 56).

HEMP SEEDS

CHIA SEEDS

FLAXSEED

BLACK SESAME
SEEDS

SESAME SEEDS

PECANS

SUNFLOWER
SEEDS

WALNUTS

ALMONDS

MACADAMIA
NUTS

HAZELNUTS

BRAZIL NUTS

CASHEWS

PISTACHIOS

SOAK AND SPROUT: Grains, Nuts, Seeds, and Legumes

Sprouts are truly "living" food! The process of soaking and sprouting at home essentially is mimicking nature's germination of a seed into a plant. Soaking nuts and seeds greatly reduces their phytic acid, a natural compound, allowing our bodies to better absorb the key nutrients like calcium, iron, magnesium, and zinc from the grains/nuts/seeds. Ounce for ounce sprouts are more nutrient rich than the older version of themselves (i.e., the seeds). Sprouts can be eaten raw, steamed, or cooked completely; you can also dehydrate the sprouted grains to make flours, such as buckwheat flour.

WHY SOAK AND/OR SPROUT?

Phytic acid is a compound, found in all legumes, grains, and nuts, that inhibits the body's absorption of certain minerals and nutrients, including iron, zinc, calcium, and B vitamins—all incredibly important and most often lacking in plant-centric diets. Soaking and sprouting nuts/seeds/grains/legumes may help increase phytase activity (phytase being an enzyme that helps break down phytic acid—a good thing). A wide range of health-related benefits have been associated with sprouted grains, including an increase in folate, vitamin C, vitamin A, B vitamins, protein content, and ease of digestibility; a reduction of common allergens (with some wheat/grains); protection from certain types of cancer (especially from broccoli sprouts); easier absorption of such minerals as iron, calcium, and zinc; and better digestion, in general, of starches, which are converted more readily into easier-to-digest simple carbohydrates.

WHAT DOES ACTIVATING NUTS AND SEEDS MEAN?

Activating nuts and seeds, or grains, is another term used for the soaking-and-sprouting process. The outer shell of many nuts and seeds will slip off after soaking; I recommend peeling off any skins that loosen during the soaking process to make blending and sprouting much easier.

HOW TO SOAK AND SPROUT

SOAK: Pour your nuts/seeds/grains/legumes in a large glass mason or sprouting-specific jar. Add water to cover by an inch or two. The precise measurement of water doesn't matter here; it's only for soaking purposes.

WAIT: Let the nuts/seeds/grains/legumes soak for the given time in the chart on page 36. Soaking times will differ depending on what you're trying to sprout.

RINSE: Rinse the nuts/seeds/grains/legumes, repeating until the water becomes clear. The process can stop here for most nuts/

seeds/grains/legumes if you simply want to use them soaked. But if you want them to sprout, continue to the next step.

SPROUT: Refer to the chart below to see how long it will take each nut/seed/grain/legume to sprout. During this sprouting phase, rinse with filtered water and drain twice a day.

GROW: As the nut/seed/grain/legume starts to sprout, you'll notice a tiny "tail" emerging. This means it's growing and sprouting! Sprouting times can vary from 1 to 4 days; you'll know it's finished when the seeds have a tail or they've sprouted greens!

STORE: Keep sprouts fresh in the refrigerator by wrapping them in a mesh cheesecloth or nut-milk bag and use within 3 or 4 days.

SOAKING AND SPROUTING TIMES

FOOD	SOAK TIME	SPROUT TIME	SPROUT LENGTH
GRAINS			
Amaranth	2–4 hours	1–1.5 days	¼ inch
Barley	8–14 hours	1–1.5 days	¼ inch
Buckwheat	15–20 min	1–1.5 days	⅛–½ inch
Corn	8–14 hours	1.5+ days	
Millet	8–14 hours	1–1.5 days	¹⁄₁₆ inch
Oats	8–14 hours	1–1.5 days	⅛ inch
Quinoa	2–4 hours	12 hours	½ inch
Rice	12–24 hours	1 day	Until the rice splits
Wheat/Rye	8–14 hours	1–1.5 days	½–¾ inch
NUTS/SEEDS			
Almonds	10–14 hours	1 day	⅛ inch
Sunflower	8–14 hours	18 hours	¼–½ inch
Cashew	2+ hours	N/A	N/A
LEGUMES			
Alfalfa	4–6 hours	5–6 days	½ inch
Chickpeas	12–18 hours	1.5+ days	½–1 inch
Lentils	8–14 hours	1 day	½–1 inch
Mung beans	8–14 hours	1 day	¼–3 inches
Peas	12–14 hours	1.5+ days	½–1 inch

Use It: Put sprouted grains in cereals and granolas, sprouted seeds in salads and sandwiches, and soaked or sprouted legumes and sprouted nuts/seeds in nut milks and cheeses; or simply eat as a crunchy snack.

MAKE A SIMPLE SALAD DRESSING

The uses for a quick no-mess, no-fuss vinaigrette are endless. In the summer, I love using pureed fresh berries, like raspberries, in a dressing; in the winter, warm vinaigrette on sautéed or roasted vegetables is delicious!

OILS:
cold-pressed sesame oil, avocado oil, walnut oil, grapeseed oil, or extra-virgin olive oil

VINEGARS/ACIDS:
raw apple cider vinegar, balsamic vinegar or balsamic reduction, red wine vinegar, rice vinegar, coconut vinegar, or any other fruit varieties of vinegar; or citrus juice, such as lemon, lime, blood orange, orange, and grapefruit

EMULSIFIERS (OPTIONAL):
yellow/spicy/honey/or Dijon mustard, egg yolk

HERBS:
fresh or dried thyme, basil, parsley, cilantro, shallots, chives

SPICES:
black pepper, cayenne pepper, turmeric, cumin, ginger, nutmeg, cinnamon

---

SIMPLE VINAIGRETTE
3 parts oil to 2 parts vinegar/acid + 1 emulsifier + your choice of fresh herbs and spices

---

1. Pour the vinegar/acid into a bowl and slowly whisk in the oil, with optional emulsifiers, until combined.

2. Add herbs and spices to taste.

3. Adjust acidity to taste.

4. Store in an airtight glass container in the refrigerator for up to 1 week. Shake to mix before using.

Use It: Dress salads or enjoy as a marinade, dipping sauce, or finishing oil.

MASSAGE KALE

Since raw kale is so dense and tough, our bodies can stand to use a little help "predigesting" it before it enters our digestive systems. Massaging kale with sea salt, lemon juice, and olive oil helps break down the cell walls of the kale, creating a more manageable bite to chew and digest; it also releases some of the chlorophyll and vitamins, turning it from a dark shade of green to a bright green—that's when you know it's finished!

1. Put 4 cups chopped raw kale in a large bowl, add the juice of 2 lemons (about ¼ cup), ½ teaspoon sea salt, and 1 tablespoon olive oil.

2. Start to massage. Pick up a handful of kale at a time, and in a circular motion, rub your fingers into it, gently bruising and breaking up the leaves.

3. Continue for about 5 minutes, or until the kale is visually brighter green and has softened.

Use It: Perfect as the base of any salad, you can also serve it as a side dish lightly sautéed with your favorite vegetables or as a topping on a sandwich/burger, or enjoy it plain.

COOK GLUTEN-FREE GRAINS

Gluten-free grains cook very similarly to non-gluten-free grains. Depending on the grain, the finished texture is fluffy and light. With amaranth, I love to "overcook" it and create a Cream of Wheat/grits texture. Although it isn't a necessity, I recommend soaking grains before cooking to help quicken the cooking process.

GRAIN	GRAIN-TO-WATER RATIO IN CUPS	COOKING DIRECTIONS
Amaranth	1:3	Boil water, add amaranth, and simmer with lid on for 20 minutes until soft.
Black rice	1:2	Wash and rinse 2 to 3 times, then drain. Cover with a tight-fitting lid, bring to a boil, reduce to simmer, and cook for 45 minutes.
Brown rice	1:3	Boil water, add brown rice, and simmer for 35 to 45 minutes.
Buckwheat groats	1:2	Boil water, add buckwheat, cook over low heat for 12 to 15 minutes, and then let stand 5 minutes.
Corn grits/ Polenta	1:5	Boil water, add grits, boil again, then reduce heat to a simmer and cook for 15 to 20 minutes.
Jasmine rice	1:1½	Bring rice and water to a boil in a pot, stir once, cover, reduce heat to low, and simmer for 18 minutes. Remove from heat and let stand, covered, for 5 minutes; fluff with a fork.
Millet	1:2	Boil water, add millet, and simmer for 15 to 20 minutes until soft.
Rolled oats	1½ to 2 cups water or milk	Boil water, pour on top of oats, and let sit for 5 minutes; or cook over medium heat until tender, about 10 minutes; or soak overnight in the refrigerator—no cooking required.
Quinoa	1:2	Boil water, add quinoa, and simmer for 15 to 20 minutes until soft.

Use It: Use grains for breakfast porridges, stir-fries, and side dishes; as a topping for salads; and as a thickener for soups.

POACH THE PERFECT EGG

Poaching an egg can be intimidating at first, but it's all in the timing and being mindful—don't walk away from the pot while it's cooking! The results are delicious and leave you with a rich egg yolk cascading over your favorite dish.

1. Pour 1 inch of water into a medium pot. Add 1 teaspoon kosher salt and 2 teaspoons distilled white vinegar or raw apple cider vinegar. Bring the water to a simmer over medium heat.

2. Use a spoon to rapidly stir the simmering water, creating a vortex and whirling motion in the water.

3. Quickly crack an egg over the pot and allow it to fall in the center. Immediately pick up your spoon again and resume whirling the water around the egg to keep the momentum going. Your spoon should not touch the egg at all; you're simply helping it stay in the middle of the pot.

4. When the egg turns white and is setting up, turn off the heat, cover the pot with a lid, and let simmer for 3 minutes for a runny yolk and 5 minutes for medium.

5. Using a spider or slotted spoon, remove the egg gently and serve.

Use It: Poached eggs are perfect on top of a bowl of cooked grains with wilted greens, on top of sautéed or roasted vegetables, and as a topping on Garden Beetroot Pizza with Sunflower Seed Pâté (page 177).

EGGS 101
I'm giving a little special attention to eggs in this section for several reasons: I use them often in recipes, they're great sources of protein and healthful fat, they add versatility by binding or adding volume to dishes, and they taste great. I always recommend getting eggs (and all animal proteins) from a local farmer or someone you know: happy chickens = happy eggs. If you're shopping, choose those that are organic, cage-free, non-GMO, and/or free range.

COOK BEANS AND LEGUMES

It's better to use dried beans and legumes rather than canned, as you'll avoid any natural or unnatural preservatives, which are added to extend the canned products' shelf life, and you'll reduce your risk for ingesting BPA. If using canned beans, which I sometimes do for convenience, I highly recommend buying organic ones that are stored in a BPA-free can. But cooking dried beans and legumes is easy.

1. Soak beans overnight in filtered water in a large bowl with enough room for the beans to slightly expand. I cover beans with a good 2 to 3 inches of water on top.

2. Drain and rinse the beans well before cooking.

3. Optional step: Sprout the beans (see page 35). If sprouting, you can eat after the bean has sprouted or continue with the cooking process.

4. Place the beans in a pot, add water to cover the beans by 1 inch, and bring to a boil.

5. Reduce the heat to a simmer and cook for 1 to 3 hours, or until fork tender; add a pinch of salt when the beans are just tender.

6. Cool, then store the beans in an airtight glass container in the refrigerator to keep their texture.

Use It: Use beans and legumes for stir-fries and side dishes, as a topping for salads, and as a thickener for soups.

TOAST NUTS AND SEEDS

Toasting nuts and seeds gives them a depth of flavor you can't achieve in any other way. When you're cooking with whole foods using simple techniques and ingredients, every layer of flavor brings a level of complexity you don't want to miss out on—and it typically takes less than 5 minutes.

1. In a dry skillet over medium heat, spread out the nuts or seeds of your choice (they may be chopped, whole, or finely ground).

2. Cook for about 1 minute, continuously moving the skillet back and forth (to and away from you) over the heat source. This generates even heat on the bottom of the pan and the constant movement will keep the nuts and seeds from burning. Nuts and seeds have oils in them that can burn quickly. Your nose always knows: pay close attention to the smell of the nut or seed—it should be light, fragrant, and enjoyable.

3. Promptly remove the nuts or seeds from the hot pan to stop the cooking. If you smell any burning odor, you're too late and must start from scratch.

Use It: Sprinkle toasted nuts and seeds on salads or soups, and use them to make nut butters and nut cheeses.

MAKE NUT AND SEED BUTTERS

Nut, seed, or combination butters will provide you with a healthful snack, and having these butters on hand will allow you to whip up any number of delicious raw recipes and desserts. Lightly toast the nuts and seeds (see opposite) before blending for enhanced flavor.

NUTS:

almonds, walnuts, pecans, Brazil nuts, cashews, pine nuts, macadamia nuts

SEEDS:

pumpkin seeds, hemp seeds, flaxseeds, sunflower seeds, sesame seeds

———————

SIMPLE NUT/SEED BUTTER

2 cups nuts/seeds + sea salt (optional)

———————

1. Place the nuts or seeds in a high-speed blender or food processor (see Tip) and blend until smooth.

2. If desired, add sea salt to taste.

3. Store in an airtight glass jar in the refrigerator for up to 2 weeks.

Use It: Put a dollop on your favorite porridge, add to desserts and smoothies for added protein and healthful fats, or spread on Artisan Seeded Bread (page 134).

Tip: If using a food processor, soak the nuts or seeds for at least 1 hour before blending. I highly recommend using a high-speed blender, ideally with a nut/seed grinder attachment. Otherwise you may add 1 tablespoon coconut oil to get the butter moving.

MAKE NUT, SEED, AND GRAIN MILKS

Making homemade nut and seed milks is not only incredibly easy: It's also comparable in price to buying them at the store; the flavor is more intense; the milk is higher in nutrient density; and there's only one ingredient in its most basic and classic form!

NUTS:

almonds, walnuts, pecans, Brazil nuts, cashews, pine nuts, macadamia nuts

SEEDS:

pumpkin seeds, hemp seeds, flaxseeds, sunflower seeds, sesame seeds/tahini paste

GRAINS:

rolled oats; soaked and sprouted white rice, brown rice, or wild rice

---

SIMPLE NUT/SEED/GRAIN MILK RECIPE

1 cup nut/seed/grain of choice + 4 cups filtered water + 1¼ teaspoons sunflower lecithin (optional, to prevent curdling)

---

1. Place the nut/seed/grain of choice, water, and sunflower lecithin (if using) in a high-speed blender. Blend until smooth.

2. Line a large serving pitcher with cheesecloth or a nut-milk bag. Gently pour in the blended nut/seed/grain mixture. Pick up the cheesecloth or nut-milk bag that's catching the pulp and gently squeeze any remaining liquid from the filter until the pulp (see Tip) is almost completely dry.

3. Store the milk in the refrigerator in an airtight glass container for 4 to 6 days.

Use It: As with any other variety of milk, dip cookies into it; add it to smoothies, porridges, cold or hot cereals, desserts, and dressings/sauces; or use it for baking.

Tip: Don't throw away the pulp! If you're making enough milk for the week, you'll have a lot of pulp. Create gluten-free nut/seed flour from the pulp by dehydrating. Set your oven to the lowest possible setting, spread the pulp on a lined baking sheet, and bake for about 8 hours, or until the flour is soft and dry. Store in an airtight glass container at room temperature for up to 2 weeks.

MAKE A VEGAN EGG REPLACEMENT

For those occasions when you're baking and need to accommodate your vegan friend or someone who doesn't eat eggs, try the following tricks. Any of the following ingredients or ingredient combinations can take the place of a single large egg.

1 tablespoon ground flaxseeds + 3 tablespoons filtered water

1 tablespoon ground chia seeds + 3 tablespoons filtered water

1 tablespoon psyllium husk + 3 tablespoons filtered water

¼ cup mashed banana (very ripe)

¼ cup applesauce

¼ cup pureed prunes

¼ cup sweet potato puree

¼ cup pumpkin puree

¼ cup blended soft tofu

¼ cup nondairy yogurt

MAKE NUT, SEED, AND GRAIN FLOURS

You've learned how to use the excess nut or seed pulp from fresh nut and seed milks to make flour; you can also make flour from the whole nuts, seeds, and grains.

SEEDS:
sunflower seeds, pumpkin seeds

NUTS:
almonds, hazelnuts, pecans, walnuts, Brazil nuts, cashews, pine nuts, pistachios

GRAINS:
rolled oats, buckwheat, quinoa, amaranth, millet, any rice variety

_____

1. Place the seeds/nuts/grains in a nut/seed grinder or clean coffee grinder and pulse for as many times as needed until the desired texture is reached. Simple as that. Just be careful not to pulse for too long, as you'll turn your flour into nut butter.

2. Store in an airtight glass container at room temperature for up to 2 weeks or in the freezer for 1 month.

Use It: These flours make delicious muffins, pancakes, waffles, cookies, and breads.

MAKE CHIA JAM

Transform any fruit of your choice with a secret ingredient, chia seeds, to make an amazing jam in less than 30 minutes—no canning required! When chia seeds mix with any liquid, they form a gel, which is the perfect texture in combination with fruit to make a fruit jam on the fly. It's higher in fiber, protein, and omega-3s than any jam you can find on market shelves and it tastes much better.

CHIA JAM

3 cups fresh or frozen fruit of your choice

2 tablespoons citrus zest

Juice of 1 lemon or orange

¼ cup pure maple syrup or honey

¼ cup chia seeds, plus 1 tablespoon as needed

Pinch of sea salt

½ teaspoon pure vanilla extract (optional)

1. Place the fruit, citrus zest, citrus juice, and maple syrup in a medium pot and bring it to a boil over medium heat.

2. Reduce the heat to a simmer and add the chia seeds. Cook for 15 to 30 minutes, until thickened, stirring occasionally. If the jam is still quite loose, add up to 1 tablespoon of chia seeds, until it's thick.

3. Remove from the heat and cool to room temperature. Store in an airtight glass container in the refrigerator for up to 2 weeks.

Use It: Spread on Artisan Seeded Bread (page 134), waffles, and pancakes, or top porridges with a dollop or two.

MAKE CASHEW CHEESE

Cashew cheese is a staple in the dairy-free kitchen—or for anyone looking to add mineral- and protein-rich cashews to their diet in a delicious way. This light, spreadable "cheese" gets its subtle tanginess from lemon and vinegar and its cheesy flavor from nutritional yeast, which is high in B vitamins and protein. For variations, gently fold in any fresh herb (think basil and rosemary) or olives, sun-dried tomatoes, shallots, or mushrooms.

CASHEW CHEESE

1 cup raw cashews (soaked for at least 2 hours)

¼ cup filtered water

¼ cup nutritional yeast

2 tablespoons freshly squeezed lemon juice

2 cloves garlic

2 tablespoons white wine or 1 tablespoon raw apple cider vinegar

½ to 1 tablespoon Dijon mustard

Sea salt and freshly ground black pepper to taste

Place the soaked cashews, water, nutritional yeast, lemon juice, garlic, wine, and mustard in a high-speed blender and blend until smooth. Add more mustard and salt and pepper to taste. Store in an airtight glass container for up to 1 week in the refrigerator—if it doesn't get eaten long before then!

Use It: Add a cheesy flavor to any entrée in this book, top salads or roasted vegetables with it, or serve it as a dip for fresh fruit or a spread for crackers and bread.

POP THE PERFECT POPCORN

Everyone needs to know how to pop the perfect batch of popcorn for a delicious fiber-rich snack or treat in the evening. This is a foolproof method.

PERFECT POPCORN

2 heaping tablespoons coconut oil

1 cup popcorn kernels, preferably organic and non–genetically modified

Pinch of sea salt

1. Heat the oil in a large and deep pot over high heat for about 30 seconds.

2. Add the popcorn kernels, cover immediately with a tight lid, and vigorously shake back and forth over the burner. This will ensure you're distributing the heat evenly, not burning any kernels, and allowing the already popped kernels to float to the top.

3. Continue moving the pot back and forth quickly and constantly until all kernels have popped, about 5 minutes. Done!

Use It: Try it as a topping on Basic Greens with Lemon-Sumac Dressing (page 142).

OPEN A FRESH YOUNG PEELED COCONUT

For all those times you don't have a machete to whack into a coconut, here's how to open up a young coconut.

1. Using a sharp knife, remove the husk (the white spongy shell) from the pointed top of the young peeled coconut, revealing the "nut," which is the brown part of the coconut.

2. You'll see three veins (i.e., lines) that meet at the top of the nut like an X that's missing one arm. Using one hand to hold the top of a butter knife in your fist, stick the point of it into one of the largest veins. With the other hand, quickly punch toward the top of your fisted hand to jam the knife into the coconut. If the knife doesn't pop the top off at the very first fast and hard tap, remove the knife and try another vein!

3. Lever the butter knife and move it parallel to the table, then wiggle it back and forth—this will pop off the very top round of the coconut, revealing the inside.

Use It: Enjoy the coconut meat and coconut water as a snack or in a smoothie, or make Coconut Milk Yogurt (page 105).

THE
RECIPES

These recipes have been created with the freshest and most naturally nourishing ingredients for your body, mostly in the form of plants. Remember back to my story? We leave nutrition dogma at the door here in the Nutrition Stripped lifestyle, so find what works for you! These recipes are versatile and flexible enough to follow whether you're vegan or paleo; in addition to their nourishing qualities, they're all gluten- and dairy-free, leaving you plenty of wiggle room to adjust to your own needs. You'll finish each meal feeling energized and satisfied but not "stuffed." And on a cellular level you'll be giving your body a daily dose of fiber, antioxidants, anti-inflammatory compounds, vitamins, minerals, and just plain goodness from the earth.

TO DRINK

JUICES AND NUT MILKS:
THE ESSENTIAL BEVERAGES

To be sipped and enjoyed, these drinks provide rapid nutrients and fuel in the easiest-to-digest form of food you can find. Since juices lack fiber (which is stripped out during the juicing process), the nutrients they contain are more rapidly absorbed through our digestive system. Juices are great for when we just want something incredibly nutrient dense on the side of a meal or to take with us when we're on the go. Many of the juice recipes I make contain less fruit and more greens or veg to keep the natural sugars low and the nutrients high.

Juices are ideal when your body needs a break from digesting heavy foods, a little reset (see page 275), or a boost of nutrients. You can also sneak extra vegetables and fruits (as in Garden Pineapple, page 63) into them. The nut and seed milks in this chapter, like the Strawberry Brazil Nut Milk (page 59), are delicious and fun ways to incorporate healthful fats, minerals, and protein into your beverages that traditional dairy milks lack. Nut and seed milks can be used just as you would any other milk. Use them in smoothies, soups, desserts, and baked goods; or enjoy as a drink to wash down German Chocolate Cake Squares (page 241).

WATERMELON HERB

SERVES 2 • This is by far one of the best warm-weather drinks, whether you're looking to beat the bloat, quench your thirst, or just use up all that leftover watermelon from a summer barbecue. The mix of fresh mint, cilantro, fresh lime juice, and watermelon is incredibly refreshing, light, and soothing to your digestion while also providing a natural zip of energy.

4 cups cubed watermelon

Juice of 2 limes

1 cup filtered water or coconut water

¼ cup fresh mint leaves

¼ cup fresh cilantro

Ice cubes

In a high-speed blender, combine the watermelon, lime juice, water, mint, and cilantro and blend until smooth. For a chilled juice, add 1 to 2 ice cubes while blending or simply serve over ice. Enjoy immediately or store in an airtight glass container in the refrigerator for up to 2 days.

Nutrition Tip: *Mint soothes digestion and watermelon contains the active compound citrulline, which helps us get rid of excess water, including the water we retain around our stomachs.*

NUT MILK, THREE WAYS

EACH RECIPE SERVES 4 OR 5 ▪ Think outside the milk carton with these nut milks that give classic flavors like strawberry, chocolate, and vanilla a twist. Brazil nuts and strawberries pack a punch with minerals like selenium and antioxidants like vitamin C, respectively, in an upgraded version of strawberry milk; fresh mint and spinach are hidden in this delicious sweet milk, providing minerals, especially iron. Lavender has a beautiful floral taste and aroma and has been shown to help reduce stress—all while drinking milk!

STRAWBERRY BRAZIL NUT

4 cups filtered water

½ cup raw Brazil nuts

1 cup fresh strawberries

2 Medjool dates, pitted

Pinch of sea salt

MINT CHOCOLATE ALMOND

4 cups filtered water

1 cup raw almonds

5 to 7 Medjool dates, pitted

2 cups fresh spinach

3 tablespoons cocoa powder

¼ cup fresh mint leaves

Pinch of sea salt

LAVENDER VANILLA CASHEW

Lavender Vanilla Syrup (recipe opposite)

4 cups filtered water

1 cup raw cashews, soaked overnight or for at least 2 hours

½ cup raw almonds

Pinch of ground cinnamon

Pinch of sea salt

For each nut-milk recipe: In a high-speed blender, combine all the ingredients and blend until smooth. Filter the pulp by following the nut-milk how-to on page 45. Serve chilled over ice or store in an airtight glass container in the refrigerator for up to 3 days.

LAVENDER VANILLA SYRUP

½ cup filtered water

1 vanilla bean pod, split lengthwise

½ cup honey

2 tablespoons lavender buds

In a small saucepan, bring the water to a boil. Scrape in the vanilla seeds and add the pod, honey, and lavender. Reduce the heat to a simmer and cook for 15 minutes, or until the mixture has thickened. Set to cool off the heat for at least 20 minutes before straining out the vanilla pod and lavender.

Nutrition Tip: Most of us rarely consume Brazil nuts, but just one Brazil nut contains more than 137 percent of the daily value for selenium, a potent antioxidant that is crucial to overall health and immune function.

KALE LEMON AND LIMEADE

SERVES 2 ▪ Give lemonade a makeover with tangy lemons, mineral-rich kale juice, and fresh ginger. To get the traditional sweetness, I use fresh homemade apple juice—no refined sugars or syrups needed here! You can use any type of apple, but I love using a green apple to make the juice a bit lower in sugar and give it more tang. Mixing greens with lemon is my number one trick when making green juices or green smoothies to help "cut" the green flavor. Plus, lemons are a great source of vitamin C, which plays perfectly well with iron- and calcium-loaded kale: Mixing vitamin C–packed foods alongside nonheme iron (a fancy way of saying plant-based sources of iron) optimizes the absorption.

1 apple, cored and halved

1-inch piece fresh ginger, peeled

4 cups chopped kale, destemmed

1 cup filtered water

Juice of 5 lemons

Juice of 2 limes

Using a juicer: Feed into the juicer half of the apple, followed by the ginger, kale, and the remaining apple half. This helps the juicer get every good green bit through it. Pour the juice into a pitcher, add the water, lemon juice, and lime juice, and stir. Serve over ice.

Using a high-speed blender: Follow the step-by-step directions on how to juice with a blender on page 32. Serve over ice.

MINERALIZING COCOA SEED MILK

SERVES 5 • Many of us, even those making conscious choices to live a healthier lifestyle, can be low in minerals because of stress, lack of sleep, poor diet, or sweating from high levels of athletic activity. This combination of seeds and cocoa powder provides ample amounts of magnesium, manganese, selenium, zinc, iron, calcium, copper, phosphorus, and potassium to replenish your body.

5 cups filtered water

1 cup raw pumpkin seeds

½ cup raw sunflower seeds

½ cup raw hemp seeds

3 tablespoons cocoa powder

2 tablespoons tahini

6 Medjool dates, pitted

1 teaspoon sea salt

Pinch of ground cinnamon

In a high-speed blender, combine the water, seeds, cocoa, tahini, dates, salt, and cinnamon and blend until smooth. If you prefer to remove the pulp, strain through cheesecloth or a nut-milk bag after blending. Serve chilled or store in an airtight glass container in the refrigerator for up to 3 days.

GARDEN PINEAPPLE

SERVES 1 • One serving of this refreshing juice contains three servings of vegetables and one serving of fruit. The yellow bell peppers and carrots are naturally sweet and add a boost of vitamins C and A. Just a small amount of pineapple gives this juice added sweetness and its gorgeous yellow color. When fresh pineapple isn't available, you can use frozen.

1 yellow bell pepper

1 large carrot

½ cup cubed fresh pineapple

½-inch piece fresh ginger, peeled

3 to 4 fresh mint leaves

1 large English (seedless) cucumber

1 lemon, peeled

Using a juicer: Run the bell pepper, carrot, and pineapple through first, followed by the ginger and mint. Feed the cucumber and lemon through the juicer last to catch any remaining bits in the juicer. Enjoy immediately or store in an airtight glass container in the refrigerator for up to 2 days or in the freezer for up to 4 days.

Using a high-speed blender: Follow the step-by-step directions on how to juice with a blender on page 32.

Nutrition Tip: Pineapple contains a natural enzyme, bromelain, which is a powerful antioxidant that helps with inflammation, muscle relaxation, and digestion.

TONICS, POTIONS, AND ELIXIRS:
THE HEALERS

C all on these exceptionally nutrient-dense beverages when your mind and body need support, healing, and a serious boost of nutrition. The queen of this section is the wildly popular Turmeric Milk from the blog, for its host of inflammation-fighting spices—including turmeric, ginger, black pepper, and cinnamon—combined with coconut milk. Sip this warm elixir several times throughout the week to manage routine inflammation or have extra during times of stress and sickness—it's delightful.

ENERGY IN A GLASS

SERVES 1 ▪ I call this Energy in a Glass because of the micronutrients in the maca powder and the bee pollen, and the natural sugar found in the dates. Maca is a root, often used in powder form, that's incredibly rich in the minerals magnesium, calcium, and iron. It's often touted as energy producing because it contains certain compounds that help strengthen stamina and focus. The B vitamins, antioxidants, anti-inflammatory compounds, and amino acids in bee pollen make it a nutrient-dense addition to any smoothie, juice, or drink.

1 cup coconut water

¼ cup light coconut milk

1 or 2 Medjool dates, pitted

1 tablespoon bee pollen granules*

1 tablespoon cocoa powder

½ tablespoon maca powder

*Purchase bee pollen granules (not in capsule form) in bulk (locally preferred) and store in your freezer for later use. Add a tablespoon to smoothies or use as a topping for oatmeal, porridge, smoothie bowls, or even desserts.

In a high-speed blender, combine the coconut water, coconut milk, dates, bee pollen granules, cocoa, and maca powder and blend until smooth. If desired, increase the sweetness by adding more dates or some honey and blend again. Blend with a couple of ice cubes or serve over ice. Enjoy immediately.

TURMERIC MILK

SERVES 2 • Meet the most famous recipe from Nutrition Stripped! Upon initially sharing this recipe, it went viral and, to this day, it is the most visited link on my blog—for good reason! I'm thrilled to see how many people are adventurous enough to take a traditional spice and use it in a unique way. Mixing almond milk with ground turmeric and warming spices—such as ginger, black pepper, cinnamon, and cardamom—and then sweetening with a touch of honey is the ultimate anti-inflammatory drink that tastes like a latte.

Turmeric contains many active components responsible for fighting inflammation, the most well known being curcumin, which has been studied for a variety of other health benefits too. Not only does this health-boosting drink decrease inflammation, it's also delicious and comforting to enjoy at night, when the weather is cold/gloomy, or whenever you're feeling a little under the weather. I "prescribe" this milk to many of my clients with inflammatory issues and they've had great success stories.

2 cups almond milk
  (see page 45), or
  full-fat coconut milk

1 tablespoon coconut oil

1 teaspoon ground turmeric

1 cinnamon stick or 1 teaspoon
  ground cinnamon

1 teaspoon grated peeled
  fresh ginger

Pinch of sea salt

Freshly ground black pepper

Honey

In a small saucepan, combine the almond milk, oil, turmeric, cinnamon stick, ginger, salt, and pepper to taste and bring to a soft boil. Reduce the heat and simmer for 10 minutes. Strain the milk through a fine-mesh strainer (discard the solids).

The oil will typically float to the top. Using a milk frother, whisk, or immersion blender, blend the oil until the turmeric milk becomes frothy. Stir in as much honey as desired to sweeten, and enjoy warm.

Tip: Make a large batch of turmeric milk for a quick drink anytime during the week and store in a glass jar in the refrigerator for no more than 3 days. Simply reheat on the stove and sweeten to taste.

Nutrition Tip: Black pepper boosts the anti-inflammatory benefits of turmeric, so don't skip out!

ELDERBERRY LIME INFUSION

SERVES 1 ▪ This infusion is a refreshing, bubbly, antioxidant-rich beverage to enjoy anytime you want to give your immune system a little boost.

1 cup sparkling water

1 tablespoon Elderberry Syrup (recipe follows)

Juice of 2 limes

Sprig of fresh rosemary

In a glass, stir together the sparkling water, elderberry syrup, and lime juice. Gently bruise the rosemary inside the glass to infuse the natural oils from the herb. You may leave the rosemary in the glass for presentation or strain it out. Serve over ice.

Nutrition Tip: Elderberries are incredibly nutrient dense, containing vitamin C, carotenoids, amino acids, flavonoids, trace minerals, potassium, calcium, and phosphorus.

ELDERBERRY SYRUP

MAKES 3 CUPS ▪ *Also known as Sambucus, elderberries have been used for centuries in medicinal tonics, sodas, and cocktails and in savory dishes—the possibilities are limitless. Fresh elderberries may be difficult to find depending on your location, so use dried if necessary. Break out the elderberry syrup during the winter months or flu season and take a spoonful for a boost of nutrients.*

4 cups filtered water
2 cups fresh elderberries or 1 cup dried
2 tablespoons grated peeled fresh ginger
1 to 2 cinnamon sticks
1 cup honey
½ teaspoon whole cloves

In a medium saucepan, combine the water, elderberries, ginger, cinnamon, honey, and cloves and bring the mixture to a boil. Cover and reduce the heat to low. Simmer for 45 to 60 minutes, until the liquid has thickened and reduced by half. Remove from the heat and let cool enough to be handled.

Pour the liquid into a high-speed blender and blend until smooth. Pour through a fine-mesh sieve into a large mason jar; you want to remove any pieces of cinnamon, berry pulp, and cloves. (Discard the pulp or compost it.) Store in an airtight glass container in the refrigerator for up to 3 months.

IMMUNITY TONIC

SERVES 2 • We all fall ill at some point during the year, whether from winter colds and flu or running ourselves down with stress. It's important to slow down, get plenty of rest, and eat well and also to boost our nutrient intake with purpose. The nutrients, antioxidants, and anti-inflammatory compounds found in the ingredients in this tonic all help strengthen the body's defenses. Pineapple and lemon are both potent sources of vitamin C; ginger, cinnamon, and cayenne are all "warming" spices, which can help break up congestion and mucus; mint is soothing to digestion, which is especially great for upset stomachs; and turmeric is my favorite anti-inflammatory spice. Add this recipe to your collection of natural remedies.

2 cups filtered water

½-inch piece fresh ginger, peeled and minced

½-inch piece fresh turmeric, peeled and minced, or 1 teaspoon ground turmeric

½ teaspoon cayenne pepper, or to taste

1 teaspoon ground cinnamon

½ teaspoon sea salt

2 cups freshly juiced pineapple

Juice of 4 lemons

2 tablespoons honey, or to taste

1 tablespoon raw apple cider vinegar (optional)

2 fresh mint leaves, for garnish

In a medium saucepan, combine the water, ginger, turmeric, cayenne, cinnamon, and salt. Simmer for 30 minutes, then remove from the heat and add the pineapple juice, lemon juice, honey, and vinegar (if using). Serve warm, with each mug topped with a fresh mint leaf. Or cool and pour over ice to serve chilled.

BEAUTY PAPAYA POTION

SERVES 1 • I call this my beauty potion because it's loaded with beautifying minerals, vitamins, and antioxidants, all aimed at playing a role in keeping your skin beautiful and your digestive system healthy and happy.

Papaya is often overlooked, yet it's one of the top fruits high in vitamin C and vitamin A—a must-have vitamin when it comes to collagen production and beautiful skin. Zinc-, iron-, and selenium-rich pumpkin seeds, Brazil nuts, and spirulina all combine together to be a phenomenal mix of nutrients vital to keeping our cells lubricated and healthy, our skin radiant and glowing. Since spirulina is a blue-green algae, get ready to see your smoothie turn dark green-blue!

1 cup pumpkin-seed milk, (see page 45)

1 cup fresh or frozen papaya cubes

1 or 2 Medjool dates, or to taste, pitted

1 Brazil nut

1 tablespoon ground flaxseeds

1 tablespoon spirulina powder

2 teaspoons maca powder

½ teaspoon pure vanilla extract

1 teaspoon chaga mushroom powder (optional)

¼ teaspoon ground cinnamon

In a high-speed blender, combine the pumpkin-seed milk, papaya, dates, Brazil nut, flaxseeds, spirulina and maca powders, vanilla, mushroom powder (if using), and cinnamon and blend until smooth. Adjust the sweetness to taste by adding more dates. Blend with 1 or 2 ice cubes or serve over ice.

MUSHROOM TONIC

SERVES 1 • Tonic: a medicinal substance taken to give a feeling of vigor or well-being. This recipe may seem intimidating to those of you who don't have a pantry stocked with high-quality freeze-dried mushroom powders, but I highly recommend that you invest in some! Because a little mushroom powder goes a long way, I've had some last an entire year while making recipes with them at least once a week. Mushrooms are known for their power-ful antioxidant, anti-inflammatory, and cancer-fighting properties, which are beneficial to consume on a regular basis; the active constituents that make these mushrooms "medici-nal" are primarily polysaccharides including beta-glucans and triterpenes.

This tonic is a unique blend of sweet, savory, and earthy flavors. The chewy dates, nutty chia seeds, and ground flaxseeds bind this drink together to create a milkshake-like texture. The ground turmeric adds another level of anti-inflammatory and antioxidant support, and blending it with the coconut oil, cocoa powder, and honey gives this tonic a unique flavor and nutrient spike.

1 cup light coconut milk, almond milk, cashew milk, or hemp milk

½ cup filtered water

1 tablespoon chia seeds

1 tablespoon ground flaxseeds

1 tablespoon melted coconut oil

1 tablespoon honey

1 or 2 Medjool dates, pitted

2 tablespoons cocoa powder

½ teaspoon ground turmeric

1½ teaspoons organic mushroom powder mix*

Pinch of sea salt

In a high-speed blender, combine the coconut milk, water, chia seeds, flaxseeds, oil, honey, dates, cocoa powder, turmeric, mushroom powder, and salt and blend until smooth. Adjust the sweetness by adding additional dates. Serve over ice or serve warm by pouring into a small saucepan and gently heating to the desired temperature.

*Find medicinal mushroom powder at your local natural foods store.

MEDICINAL MUSHROOMS

Mushrooms have been used medicinally for centuries to calm the nervous system, help fight bacteria and viruses, and help boost the immune system. Medicinal mushrooms are *packed* with antioxidants and anti-inflammatory compounds, and studies show that the active constituents in these mushrooms have immune-boosting properties, among other health benefits.

My favorite of the mushrooms, thanks to their flavor, use, and nutrients are reishi, shiitake, chaga, maitake, king oyster, and *Cordyceps*. Many, if not all, of these mushrooms are also loaded with B vitamins, zinc, manganese, choline, dietary fiber, vitamin D, copper, antioxidants, anti-inflammatory compounds, and more. You can make your own mix by combining any of the above-mentioned mushrooms. For a more budget-friendly option, see page 289 for my favorite mixes.

MORNING
STORIES

SMOOTHIES AND SMOOTHIE BOWLS:
INSTANT ENERGY BOOST

My favorite kind of recipe to create is smoothies and smoothie bowls. They're completely nourishing and full of fiber, which keeps our digestive systems happy and efficient. The Stripped Green Smoothie (page 82) is nutrient dense and supports your body's detoxification on a daily basis. If you're new to green smoothies, try Citrus Creamy Ginger Green Smoothie (page 80).

Smoothie bowls, which have been a huge hit on the Nutrition Stripped blog, are innovative ways to enjoy smoothies: They are thick enough to eat with a spoon (think ice cream) and are often topped with a variety of "superfoods": granolas (such as The Best Chocolate Granola, page 121), nuts, seeds, or fresh fruits.

The amazing thing about smoothies and smoothie bowls is how easy they are to adapt to your taste. Add in what you love and omit what you don't. The recipes in this chapter also mix it up with nontraditional ingredients. Yes, sweet potatoes in your smoothie like the Sweet Potato Julius (page 90) or frozen zucchini to thicken any smoothie without adding heaps of sugar. Cheers to starting your morning light, refreshed, and invigorated.

CITRUS CREAMY GINGER GREEN SMOOTHIE

SERVES 1 ▪ This is the ultimate green smoothie for people who don't yet *love* green smoothies. Readers went wild over this velvety smoothie when I first introduced it. Not only do avocado and tahini taste amazing together, they're both loaded with healthful fats and bone-strengthening minerals, such as potassium, magnesium, copper, zinc, phosphorus, calcium, iron, and manganese. The spinach is a great source of vitamin K, which plays an important role in keeping our bones strong. All of these whole-food ingredients are a match made in bone-health heaven.

1 cup filtered water

3 cups fresh spinach

1 medium banana

½ medium or 1 small avocado

1 tablespoon tahini

½- to 1-inch piece fresh ginger, peeled

2 Medjool dates, pitted

Juice of 1 lemon

Juice of 1 lime

In a high-speed blender, combine the water, spinach, banana, avocado, tahini, ginger, dates, and lemon and lime juices and blend until smooth and creamy. Blend with 1 or 2 ice cubes or serve over ice. Store in an airtight glass container in the refrigerator for up to 1 day.

Low-sugar variation: Omit the banana and dates and use 1 whole medium avocado and 1 tablespoon chia seeds. Sweeten with stevia to taste.

STRIPPED GREEN SMOOTHIE

SERVES 2 TO 4 • Drinking greens can be an odd idea for most of us to grasp, yet the benefits of drinking this smoothie are something that must be felt and experienced for yourself. This recipe encompasses what the Nutrition Stripped lifestyle is all about—getting creative by using whole-food ingredients in innovative ways, packing them with nutrition, and making them taste delicious.

Adding raw greens to smoothies is not only a way to boost the fiber content in our diets, but it also squeezes in extra minerals and plant proteins that are often overlooked. Its unique ingredients set this green smoothie apart from the rest—cilantro, parsley, turmeric, cinnamon, ginger, Brazil nuts, and cayenne pepper. All these ingredients contribute to the unique flavor and they each serve a purpose: The cinnamon helps stabilize blood sugar, turmeric is a powerful anti-inflammatory spice, and cilantro and parsley are natural diuretics that help detoxify our bodies by flushing out excess fluid. The selenium in Brazil nuts plays an important role in thyroid and metabolic function, and fresh ginger and cayenne are warming spices that fire up our metabolism from the inside out and give this smoothie a kick of heat!

Just one smoothie contains one-third of your daily requirement for fiber, as well as vitamins A, K, and C; B vitamins; iron; potassium; zinc; selenium; calcium; magnesium; phytonutrients; antioxidants; and anti-inflammatory compounds. I've had countless clients, readers, and women in the Nutrition Stripped community tell me how much better they felt when incorporating the Stripped Green Smoothie into their daily morning routine. From endless energy that rivals the effects of any cup of coffee to improved digestion and regular trips to the bathroom, to glowing skin, to better mental and physical performance, I've experienced these shifts as well and it's the reason this recipe is a staple in my diet. I drink it almost every single day!

2 cups filtered water

5 large stalks celery, chopped

1 large head romaine lettuce, chopped

1 large bunch of lacinato kale, destemmed (see Note) and chopped

1 cup coconut water

1 large sweet apple, such as Fuji, cored and chopped

2 medium bananas, chopped

½ cup chopped cucumber

½ cup fresh cilantro

½ cup fresh parsley leaves

Juice of 1 lemon

Juice of 1 lime

4 Brazil nuts

½-inch piece fresh ginger, peeled

Dash of cayenne pepper

Dash of ground cinnamon

Dash of ground turmeric

In a high-speed blender, combine the water, celery, and lettuce. Puree on low speed. Gradually increase the speed to high and add the kale. Add the coconut water, apple, bananas, cucumber, cilantro, parsley, citrus juices, Brazil nuts, ginger, cayenne, cinnamon, and turmeric and blend until creamy. Blend with 1 or 2 ice cubes or serve over ice. Store in an airtight glass container in the refrigerator for up to 4 days.

Note: *To destem greens quickly: Grip the end of the stem with your nondominant hand. Place your dominant index finger and middle finger on either side of the stem and run them down the stem, stripping the leaves while your other hand provides opposing force.*

Low-sugar variation: *Use filtered water for the coconut water, omit the bananas, and substitute a green apple for the sweet one.*

AÇAÍ BERRY BOWL

SERVES 1 OR 2 • This smoothie bowl is made with a mixture of sweet frozen strawberries and bananas, açaí, and delicious and fun toppings to garnish it with! I love enjoying açaí bowls especially in the warmer months of the year when my body naturally craves cooler foods to start the day; it's one of my favorite morning meals. Have fun with the garnishes: Every bowl can be unique and change during the seasons! To boost the protein, add a scoop of your favorite plant-based protein powder, nut butter, or hemp seeds, or my favorite, spirulina (which will turn this smoothie blue!).

1 (3.5-ounce) packet frozen açaí berry pulp*

1 cup frozen strawberries

½ frozen banana

½ cup cashew milk (see page 45)

2 tablespoons chia seeds

Dash of ground cinnamon

Garnishes: chopped raw almonds, unsweetened shredded coconut, cacao nibs, sliced fresh banana, The Best Chocolate Granola (page 121), bee pollen, hemp seeds, chia seeds, sliced fresh strawberries

Find frozen açaí berry pulp at your local natural foods store or online.

In a high-speed blender, combine the açaí berry pulp, strawberries, banana, cashew milk, chia seeds, and cinnamon and blend until smooth. The texture should be like that of soft-serve ice cream or pudding; adjust the cashew milk accordingly, or add ice to thicken to your preference. Pour into a serving bowl and garnish as desired.

Low-sugar variation: Use ½ cup frozen strawberries and ¼ frozen banana and add 1 cup frozen zucchini or frozen green peas.

REPLENISH SMOOTHIE

SERVES 1 ▪ I created this smoothie with one thing in mind: fuel. Whether you're refueling after an intense workout session or looking for a meal with energy to last several hours, this one's got you covered. The combination of kiwi, banana, spinach, avocado, dates, zucchini, almond butter, coconut milk, and lime juice contains enough electrolytes and minerals to replenish any lost during exercise. One smoothie also contains two servings each of vegetables and fruit, all aimed at keeping your metabolism and energy humming along. To boost the protein, add a scoop of your favorite plant-based protein powder.

2 cups fresh spinach

1 medium zucchini, cut up

½ cup light coconut milk

½ cup filtered water

½ banana

1 kiwi, unpeeled (see Tip)

¼ avocado

1 tablespoon almond butter (see page 43)

1 Medjool date, pitted

Juice of 1 lime

In a high-speed blender, combine the spinach, zucchini, coconut milk, water, banana, kiwi, avocado, almond butter, date, and lime juice and blend until thick and creamy. Adjust the texture by adding more water or coconut milk to thin. Blend with 1 or 2 ice cubes or serve over ice. Enjoy immediately.

Nutrition Tip: The skin of the kiwi, which is more commonly peeled off and discarded, is actually completely edible and contains a wide variety of nutrients—why not blend it?

BEETROOT PINK SMOOTHIE BOWL

SERVES 1 ▪ Beets are responsible for the lovely pink color in this smoothie bowl and are a great ingredient to incorporate into our diets for anti-inflammatory and detoxification benefits. The phytonutrients (betalains) in beets help support our metabolic detoxification process. The zucchini bulks this smoothie up with fiber and volume without adding sugar or many calories—win, win! If raw beets are too strong for your taste, roast them at 400°F for 40 minutes, or until soft, for a naturally sweeter taste. To boost the protein, add a scoop of your favorite plant-based protein powder.

½ to ⅔ cup cashew milk (see page 45)

2 small beets, peeled and chopped

1 cup frozen raspberries

½ medium pear, cored

½ cup frozen chopped zucchini

1 Medjool date, pitted

Juice of 1 lemon

½-inch piece fresh ginger, peeled

Garnishes: The Best Chocolate Granola (page 121), cacao nibs, sliced fresh strawberries, sliced fresh banana, unsweetened shredded coconut, bee pollen

In a high-speed blender, combine ½ cup of the cashew milk, the beets, raspberries, pear, zucchini, date, lemon juice, and ginger and blend until smooth. Adjust the texture by using more cashew milk for a thinner smoothie (for drinking through a straw) or thicken by adding more frozen zucchini or frozen raspberries (for eating with a spoon in a smoothie bowl). Garnish as desired.

Tip: Using fresh or frozen chopped zucchini in your smoothies will make them creamy without adding sugar or fat. Keep chopped zucchini in your freezer for an easy addition to all your smoothies.

SWEET POTATO JULIUS

SERVES 1 ▪ The first "real" recipe I ever tried was for the famous orange Julius. It was back in home-ec class and the no-fail recipe instantly became my favorite. Now I'm giving traditional orange Julius an upgrade by combining the vitamins C and A, potassium, fiber, and carotenoids found in sweet potatoes with tangy orange. This is a winning combination, light and refreshing with pops of citrus, yet dense and filling because of the sweet potato. Enjoy this as a meal or postworkout drink, or split it with a loved one for a snack! It's ridiculously good.

1 cup almond milk
(see page 45)

1 medium sweet potato,
baked whole

1 medium orange, peeled

1 Medjool date, or to taste,
pitted

1 teaspoon pure vanilla extract

Dash of sea salt

Dash of ground cinnamon

Honey (optional)

In a high-speed blender, combine the almond milk, sweet potato, orange, date, vanilla, salt, and cinnamon and blend until smooth. Adjust the sweetness to your desired taste by adding honey or more Medjool dates. Blend in about ½ cup ice to chill before serving.

Tip: This recipe offers the perfect example of how batch cooking comes in handy: Baking up a batch of sweet potatoes to have them ready for use in any application is such a time saver!

MANGO AND TURMERIC GOLDEN LASSI

SERVES 2 ▪ A traditional Indian yogurt drink made with dairy, fruit, and spices, lassi can be enjoyed both sweet and savory. The ever-popular mango is the perfect sweet complement to the rich, earthy, and deep flavor of turmeric. When blended with coconut milk yogurt, both mango and turmeric create a beautiful golden color. The warming spices nutmeg, cinnamon, and cardamom provide balance and make this a borderline sweet/savory yogurt drink.

Flesh from 1 mango, pitted and peeled

1 cup Coconut Milk Yogurt (page 105)

1 cup almond milk (see page 45)

1 teaspoon ground turmeric

2 tablespoons pure maple syrup (optional)

Seeds from 1 vanilla bean pod, split lengthwise

Pinch of freshly grated nutmeg

Pinch of ground cardamom

Pinch of ground cinnamon

Pinch of sea salt

In a high-speed blender, combine the mango, yogurt, almond milk, turmeric, and maple syrup (if using). Scrape in the vanilla seeds and add the nutmeg, cardamom, cinnamon, and salt and blend until smooth. Adjust the seasoning by adding more turmeric or, for sweetness, maple syrup. Serve chilled or store in an airtight glass container in the refrigerator for up to 2 days.

Nutrition Tip: Mango is a great source of vitamin C and turmeric is high in anti-inflammatory compounds. Together, they make a great duo for combating inflammation and providing antioxidants. The beneficial bacteria in the yogurt and the fiber in the fruit aid in digestion.

GOLDEN GINGER HONEY SMOOTHIE

SERVES 1 OR 2 • I developed this smoothie out of a need for something completely sooth-ing on my digestion after a long week of traveling and holidays had thrown off my normal eating habits. Ginger soothes our digestive systems and helps curb nausea. It's strong in flavor, so adjust to your liking. This beautiful golden-yellow smoothie also contains honey (a natural antimicrobial), inflammation-fighting turmeric, and fiber-packed vitamin A–rich carrot and sweet potato.

1 cup almond milk
(see page 45)

4 large carrots, chopped and
steamed until soft

3 ounces baked sweet potato
(from about ½ medium)

1 orange, peeled

Juice of 1 lemon

1 teaspoon ground turmeric

2 tablespoons honey

½-inch piece fresh ginger,
peeled

Pinch of sea salt

In a high-speed blender, combine the almond milk, steamed carrots, sweet potato, orange, lemon juice, turmeric, honey, ginger, and salt and blend until smooth. Serve over ice or enjoy at room temperature.

Creamier option: Use light coconut milk instead of almond milk.

Sweeter option: Add 1 or 2 Medjool dates for a little more sweetness.

———

Nutrition Tip: Both carrots and sweet potatoes contain vitamin A (carotenoids), which actually increases when cooked!

CHOCOLATE COCONUT CHIP SMOOTHIE

SERVES 1 OR 2 • This smoothie is a crowd-pleaser. It's made with whole-food ingredients that make it feel like a traditional down-home milkshake and that's my goal—sometimes you just want a milkshake! This smoothie is great as a sweet snack or dessert, and staying true to my whole-living philosophy, it contains medium-chain triglycerides (i.e., healthful fats) from the coconut milk, carbohydrates and fiber from the banana, and antioxidants from both the cocoa powder and cacao nibs. To boost the protein, add a scoop of your favorite plant-based protein powder.

1 cup light coconut milk

1 banana

2 tablespoons cocoa powder

2 tablespoons unsweetened shredded coconut

2 tablespoons cacao nibs or ½ tablespoon cocoa powder

1 tablespoon almond butter (see page 43)

¼ teaspoon pure vanilla extract

Pinch of sea salt

In a high-speed blender, combine the coconut milk, banana, cocoa powder, coconut, cacao nibs, almond butter, vanilla, and salt and blend until smooth. Blend with 1 or 2 ice cubes or serve over ice. Add additional cacao nibs and coconut shreds to garnish, if desired.

BREAKFAST:
A NEW WAY TO
FUEL YOUR MORNING

B reaking the fast, literally. Breakfast fuels our bodies with energy for the day; it kick-starts our digestive systems, focuses our brains, and revs our metabolism. It's also the meal that can be enjoyed in silence and savored as your mind, body, and spirit slowly wake. Many of these recipes are easy to make, like Buckwheat Bircher Muesli, Three Ways (page 111), for when you need to fuel up and get out the door. Others, like Coconut Milk Yogurt (page 105) and Lemon Donuts with Strawberry Beetroot Glaze (page 100), are perfect for cozy weekend mornings. Try to make breakfast part of your daily routine, even if it's a simple bowl of fresh fruit with a hot cup of tea: Your mind and body will respond with clarity and energy.

PLANTAIN FLATBREAD WITH POACHED EGG AND HONEY DRIZZLE

SERVES 1 OR 2 • Think of plantains as the sister to the banana. They're not as sweet, as they contain less sugar. They're also higher in starch than most fruits, making them perfect for gluten- and grain-free breads. My favorite part of this entire dish is upon serving: The moment you break the egg white just enough for the golden yolk to spill over, the starchy flatbread soaks up every last bit, leaving you with a nice balance of moisture. The egg yolk is rich and bold, with the added bonus of sprinkled salt and drizzled honey—there's nothing like it.

1 medium green/slightly yellow plantain, peeled and cut up

3 or 4 eggs

Sea salt

Freshly ground black pepper

Honey

Garnish: thinly sliced chives

Preheat the oven to 375°F. Grease a 9 × 9-inch baking pan with coconut oil.

In a high-speed blender, combine the plantain, 2 of the eggs, and a pinch of salt and blend until smooth.

Pour this mixture into the baking pan and bake for 25 to 30 minutes, until set and a toothpick inserted into the center comes out clean (or lift up the sides to check for doneness).

Poach 1 or 2 eggs (depending on how many you are serving), following the how-to on page 40. Serve the plantain flatbread topped with the poached egg(s). Sprinkle with salt and pepper to taste, and a drizzle of honey. Garnish as desired.

CHAMOMILE TEA SCONES

SERVES 8 • Incorporating tea leaves into baked goods was something I was inspired to do by one of my favorite local coffee shops here in Nashville—Barista Parlor—which is constantly serving up macaroons that are infused with tea flavors. The chamomile tea plays a fun role in these scones: Not only do you get the subtle taste of tea without having to dip these scones into a hot mug, but you also get some of the antioxidants and added minerals found in the chamomile leaves, since they are baked right in.

¼ cup loose-leaf chamomile leaves

1¾ cups gluten-free all-purpose flour

½ cup brown rice flour, (see page 47)

3 tablespoons coconut sugar

2 teaspoons baking powder

½ teaspoon baking soda

¼ teaspoon sea salt

½ cup coconut oil, melted

½ cup full-fat coconut milk, chilled

½ teaspoon pure vanilla extract

Juice of 1 lemon

2 tablespoons olive oil

For serving (optional): Chia Jam (page 48), fresh berries, Coconut Milk Yogurt (page 105), Sweet Cashew Cream (page 104)

Preheat the oven to 400°F. Line a baking sheet with parchment paper.

In a spice grinder, or with a mortar and pestle, grind the chamomile leaves until fine. You should have about 2 tablespoons ground leaves.

In a large bowl, sift together the flours, coconut sugar, baking powder, baking soda, salt, and ground chamomile leaves. Add the melted coconut oil, coconut milk, vanilla, and lemon juice and gently fold together until combined—don't overmix.

Lightly flour a work surface and roll out the dough into an 8-inch round, about ½ inch thick. Using a sharp knife, slice the dough into eight wedges. Place the wedges on the prepared baking sheet and lightly brush the tops with the olive oil. Bake the scones for 15 minutes, or until they're golden and risen.

Serve warm with jam, berries, coconut yogurt, or cashew cream, or plain with a hot mug of tea.

LEMON DONUTS WITH STRAWBERRY BEETROOT GLAZE

MAKES 8 DONUTS • Growing up, I loved cake donuts. Later, when I eliminated gluten from my diet, I didn't come across a donut I actually enjoyed until experimenting with beets led me to my personal favorite. These donuts are cakey, dense, and not cloyingly sweet. In comparison to traditional donuts, these are higher in fiber and contain minerals, protein, and healthful fats. The glaze is made with a combination of coconut oil (rich in medium-chain triglycerides) and coconut butter, and it is sweetened naturally with maple syrup, strawberries, and lightly colored and flavored with earthy beets.

LEMON DONUTS

- ½ cup oat flour
- ½ cup brown rice flour (see page 47)
- 2 tablespoons coconut flour
- 2 tablespoons almond flour (see page 47)
- 2 tablespoons ground flaxseeds
- 1 teaspoon baking powder
- ½ teaspoon baking soda
- ½ teaspoon sea salt
- ½ teaspoon ground cinnamon
- ½ cup almond milk (see page 45)
- 2 tablespoons grated fresh lemon zest
- Juice of 1 lemon
- ¼ cup pureed pear
- 3 tablespoons grapeseed oil
- ¼ cup pure maple syrup
- 1 teaspoon pure vanilla extract
- 2 teaspoons pure lemon extract

BEETROOT GLAZE

- 1 cup roasted beets (1 large or 2 small)
- 1 cup coconut butter, melted
- 1 cup fresh strawberries
- 1 tablespoon pure maple syrup
- 1 or 2 tablespoons unsweetened almond milk (see page 45)
- Pinch of ground cinnamon
- Pinch of sea salt
- Garnishes: Freeze-dried strawberries, grated fresh lemon zest

For the lemon donuts: Preheat the oven to 350°F. Grease 8 cavities of a donut pan with coconut oil. (If your donut pan has only 6 cavities, bake in two batches.)

In a large bowl, combine the flours, flaxseeds, baking powder, baking soda, salt, and cinnamon and stir to combine. In a small bowl, combine the almond milk, lemon zest, lemon juice, pureed pear, grapeseed oil, maple syrup, vanilla, and lemon extract. Pour the wet mixture into the flour mixture and stir to combine.

Pour this dough into a gallon-size resealable bag, pushing the dough to one corner of the bag. Snip a corner of the bag to make a ¼-inch hole.

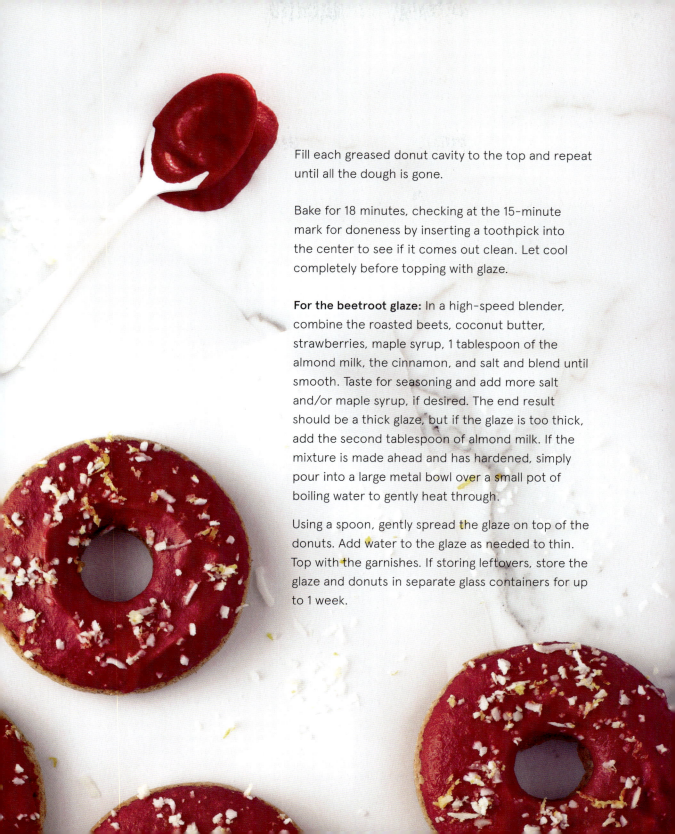

Fill each greased donut cavity to the top and repeat until all the dough is gone.

Bake for 18 minutes, checking at the 15-minute mark for doneness by inserting a toothpick into the center to see if it comes out clean. Let cool completely before topping with glaze.

For the beetroot glaze: In a high-speed blender, combine the roasted beets, coconut butter, strawberries, maple syrup, 1 tablespoon of the almond milk, the cinnamon, and salt and blend until smooth. Taste for seasoning and add more salt and/or maple syrup, if desired. The end result should be a thick glaze, but if the glaze is too thick, add the second tablespoon of almond milk. If the mixture is made ahead and has hardened, simply pour into a large metal bowl over a small pot of boiling water to gently heat through.

Using a spoon, gently spread the glaze on top of the donuts. Add water to the glaze as needed to thin. Top with the garnishes. If storing leftovers, store the glaze and donuts in separate glass containers for up to 1 week.

BLACKBERRY SUMAC SUNFLOWER SEED MUFFINS WITH CITRUS CREAM

MAKES 12 MUFFINS • I enjoy making healthier versions of classically carbohydrate-laden foods while boosting the healthful fats and protein, and this recipe is a perfect example of how to do so. These muffins are delightfully dense, chewy, and nutty, with bright flavors of tart blackberries and citrus that help cut the heaviness of the sunflower seeds and walnuts. Plus, they're incredibly simple to make. Enjoy the citrus cream topping as you would a spread of butter—it's heavenly!

1 cup raw sunflower seeds

¼ cup walnuts

¼ cup rolled oats

1 teaspoon baking powder

1 teaspoon ground sumac

½ teaspoon sea salt

¼ cup coconut oil

¼ cup honey

1 cup blackberries, pureed

2 tablespoons grated fresh orange zest

5 egg whites

Citrus Cream (recipe follows), for serving

Preheat the oven to 350°F. Grease 12 cups of a muffin tin with coconut oil.

For the muffins: In a dry skillet, toast the sunflower seeds and walnuts over medium heat until fragrant, about 2 minutes. Use a food processor, nut grinder, or high-speed blender to grind the sunflower seeds, walnuts, and oats into a fine flour. Transfer to a large bowl and stir in the baking powder, sumac, and salt.

In a large bowl, stir the coconut oil to melt it and add the honey and blackberry puree. Add the blackberry mixture and orange zest to the flour mixture and stir to combine.

In a separate large bowl, beat the egg whites until foamy. Gently fold the egg whites into the flour mixture until combined—this creates a lighter muffin. Drop about 2 tablespoons of batter into each muffin cup and repeat until the batter is completely distributed. Let the batter rest for 5 minutes before baking.

(recipe continues)

(recipe continued from previous page)

Bake for about 20 minutes, rotating the muffin tin halfway through, until the muffins are golden on the outside and a toothpick inserted into the center comes out clean. Be careful not to overbake; they'll continue to cook as they cool and should become firm.

Serve the muffins warm with a spread of citrus cream on top. Store leftover muffins in an airtight glass container in the freezer for up to 1 month. Store the cream separately in an airtight glass container in the refrigerator for up to 1 week.

—————

CITRUS CREAM
MAKES ABOUT 1½ CUPS

    1 cup raw cashews, soaked for 2 hours
 ½ cup filtered water
    1 small clementine, peeled
        Juice of 1 lemon
        Pinch of sea salt

In a high-speed blender, combine the soaked cashews, water, clementine, lemon juice, and salt and blend until smooth. Adjust the lemon juice to taste.

Sweet Cashew Cream: Omit the clementine and lemon juice and add 2 pitted dates. Adjust to taste.

—————

COCONUT MILK YOGURT

SERVES 2 TO 4 ▪ Despite what you might think about the laborious act of making your own yogurt, I promise you this one is a cinch! Just mix together the ingredients and let the good bacteria from the probiotics take over and do their work. Probiotics and naturally fermented foods are essential to a well-functioning digestive system, and this rich, flavorful yogurt tastes amazing.

1 cup full-fat coconut milk

1 cup coconut meat (from about 1 fresh young coconut; see Note)

¼ to ¾ cup coconut water (use more for thinner yogurt)

4 probiotic capsules (see page 288), opened and powder emptied into a small bowl

Juice of 1 lemon

1 teaspoon honey

Pinch of sea salt

Garnishes: honey, fresh berries, fresh figs, granola, pinch of cinnamon, pinch of nutmeg, dollop of nut butter; or savory garnishes such as olive oil, black pepper, salt, zucchini ribbons, Curry Granola (page 214)

In a high-speed blender, combine the coconut milk, coconut meat, coconut water, probiotics, lemon juice, honey, and salt and blend until smooth. Pour into one 16-ounce, two 8-ounce, or four 4-ounce sterile glass jars and seal tightly. Store at room temperature for 24 hours, during which time the yogurt will ferment. After 24 hours, if you'd like to serve the yogurt chilled, refrigerate before serving. Serve with garnishes of your choosing. Store leftover yogurt in an airtight glass container in the refrigerator for up to 1 week.

Note: Coconut meat is the white flesh from the inside of a young coconut. Follow instructions on how to open a coconut on page 51, and then scoop out the meat. Coconut meat may also be found in the frozen section of your local natural foods store.

BUCKWHEAT STACKS
WITH THREE TOPPINGS

SERVES 4 ▪ For some reason, I crave pancakes with a steaming cup of tea on weekend mornings. These may just become your favorite stackable pancake to revisit every weekend. Despite its name, buckwheat contains no wheat—it's technically a seed and is related to the rhubarb family. Buckwheat pancakes are satisfying without making you feel weighed down and contribute a macronutrient balance of carbohydrates, fiber, protein, and healthful fats.

2 cups buckwheat groats, finely ground into a flour (see page 47), or 1½ cups buckwheat flour

1 tablespoon ground flaxseeds

1 teaspoon baking soda

1 teaspoon baking powder

1 teaspoon ground cinnamon

2 eggs

1 cup almond milk (see page 45)

3 tablespoons pure maple syrup

1 teaspoon pure vanilla extract

2 tablespoons poppy seeds

1 tablespoon grated fresh lemon zest

Juice of 1 lemon

Toppings: Blueberry Compote, Roasted Plums, or Coconut Honey Cream (recipes follow)

Coconut oil, for cooking the pancakes

In a large bowl, combine the buckwheat flour, ground flaxseeds, baking soda, baking powder, and cinnamon. In a separate large bowl, combine the eggs, almond milk, maple syrup, and vanilla. Pour the wet mixture into the dry ingredients and stir to combine. Stir in the poppy seeds, lemon zest, and lemon juice. Let the batter sit for 20 minutes to allow the oats to absorb the liquid.

Meanwhile, prepare your desired topping before cooking the pancakes.

Once your topping has been prepared, grease a cast-iron skillet with just enough coconut oil to cover the bottom of the pan and heat over medium heat. Pour ⅓ cup batter onto the skillet and let cook for about 2 minutes, or until bubbles release on the top. Flip and cook for another 2 minutes, or until the pancake is firm to the touch. Repeat with the remaining batter. Dollop each pancake with the desired topping while still warm.

Both the pancakes and toppings keep well in an airtight glass container in the refrigerator for up to

(recipe continues)

(recipe continued from previous page)

4 to 5 days, or individually wrapped in foil if freezing. When ready to serve, reheat the pancakes in a toaster oven or microwave until warm, or enjoy chilled for a snack on the go.

BLUEBERRY COMPOTE

MAKES ABOUT 2 CUPS

2 cups frozen blueberries (or raspberries for low-sugar option)
½ cup filtered water
2 tablespoons pure maple syrup
Pinch of sea salt

In a small saucepan, combine the blueberries, water, maple syrup, and salt and bring to a simmer over medium-low heat. Simmer for about 20 minutes to reduce and thicken.

ROASTED PLUMS

MAKES ABOUT 1 CUP

4 plums, pitted and quartered
2 tablespoons olive oil
Sea salt

Preheat the oven to 400°F. On a baking sheet, toss the plums with the olive oil and bake for about 40 minutes, or until the natural sugars start to caramelize. Season with salt to taste.

COCONUT HONEY CREAM

MAKES 1¼ CUPS

¾ cup honey
¼ cup coconut oil
¼ cup coconut butter

In a high-speed blender, combine the honey, coconut oil, and coconut butter and blend until smooth. Transfer to a saucepan and warm over low heat.

SUPER SEED CEREAL

SERVES 14 • This classic recipe from my blog has won the hearts of many; it's Cereal 3.0 and completely celebrates the nutritional power of a variety of seeds. Super Seed Cereal can be enjoyed as a cold cereal by soaking overnight in almond milk or other nondairy milk of your choice, or it can be cooked with water or nut/seed milks. Either way you choose, you're in for a nutrient-dense cereal with healthful fats and carbohydrates to fuel your day.

2 cups buckwheat groats

1 cup hemp seeds

1 cup chia seeds

1 cup amaranth

1 cup quinoa

½ cup raw pumpkin seeds, coarsely chopped

½ cup raw sunflower seeds

Garnishes: fresh berries, pinch of cinnamon, honey

In a large bowl, stir together the buckwheat groats, hemp seeds, chia seeds, amaranth, quinoa, pumpkin seeds, and sunflower seeds. Store in an airtight glass container at room temperature for up to 3 months.

To prepare raw: In a bowl, combine ½ cup cereal and 1 cup liquid of your choice (water, almond milk, etc.), depending on desired thickness. Soak for at least 20 minutes and enjoy raw. Serve topped with a garnish of your choice.

To prepare cooked: In a small saucepan, combine ½ cup cereal and 2 cups liquid of your choice (water, almond milk, etc.) and cook for 20 minutes, or until tender. Serve topped with a garnish of your choice.

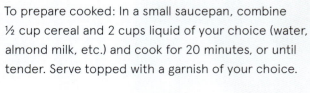

BUCKWHEAT BIRCHER MUESLI, THREE WAYS

EACH RECIPE SERVES 1 • Break out of your oatmeal rut with these buckwheat variations on overnight oats. The Citrus Honey version is light and refreshing with lemon juice and toasted coconut. Vanilla Bean Super Seed is a classic, with an added bonus of my favorite omega-3-rich seeds: hemp, chia, and flax. Savory Olive Oil is a must-try that will get you thinking outside the box when it comes to morning recipes.

SAVORY OLIVE OIL

- 1 cup light coconut milk or almond milk (see page 45)
- ¼ cup buckwheat groats or ½ cup rolled oats
- Pinch of sea salt
- Toppings (optional): ¼ cup Roasted Chickpeas (recipe follows), ¼ cup golden raisins, 1 tablespoon extra-virgin olive oil, ½ tablespoon chopped fresh thyme, drizzle of honey

VANILLA BEAN SUPER SEED

- 1 cup light coconut milk
- ¼ cup buckwheat groats or ½ cup rolled oats
- 2 tablespoons chia seeds
- 1 tablespoon hemp seeds
- 1 tablespoon ground flaxseeds
- ¼ vanilla bean pod, split lengthwise (scrape seeds into bowl)
- Pinch of sea salt
- Topping (optional): drizzle of honey

CITRUS HONEY

- 1 cup light coconut milk
- ¼ cup buckwheat groats or ½ cup rolled oats
- 1 tablespoon grated fresh lemon zest
- Juice of 1 lemon
- ¼ cup unsweetened shredded coconut
- Pinch of sea salt
- Toppings (optional): drizzle of honey, toasted shredded coconut, grated lemon zest

For each recipe: In a small serving bowl, combine all the ingredients (except the toppings) and stir until combined. Let rest at room temperature for at least 2 hours or overnight. The groats will become tender.

Serve at room temperature or refrigerate to enjoy chilled. Garnish with the optional toppings. Save leftovers in an airtight glass container in the refrigerator for up to 3 days.

ROASTED CHICKPEAS

Preheat the oven to 400°F. Line a baking sheet with parchment paper.

Drain and rinse well 2 cups canned chickpeas, spread evenly on the prepared baking sheet, and toss with 1 tablespoon olive oil and sea salt and pepper to taste. Bake for 30 to 40 minutes, until crisp. Store in an airtight glass jar at room temperature for up to 1 week.

CARROT CAKE QUINOA PORRIDGE

SERVES 4 ▪ My brother always jokes that the cake I happen to love the most is made from a vegetable, and it's completely true. This quinoa porridge is a play on carrot cake, with all the basic ingredients of a traditional carrot cake: shredded carrots, raisins, maple syrup, and warming spices like cinnamon. The best part of carrot cake is the creamy frosting that is traditionally made with cream cheese, but to make this dairy-free, I serve it with a "nut cream" made of naturally sweet nuts mixed with citrus juice to brighten up the flavor.

½ cup golden raisins

Juice of 1 orange

Juice of 1 lemon

2 cups filtered water

1 cup white quinoa

1 teaspoon ground cinnamon

¼ teaspoon freshly grated nutmeg

Pinch of sea salt

2 cups shredded carrots

2 tablespoons honey

1 teaspoon pure vanilla extract

Macadamia Nut Cream (recipe follows), for serving

In a small bowl, combine the raisins, orange juice, and lemon juice and set aside to soak.

In a medium saucepan, bring the water to a boil over high heat. Add the quinoa, cinnamon, nutmeg, and salt. Reduce to medium heat and simmer for 15 minutes.

Remove from the heat, stir in the shredded carrots, cover, and set aside for 10 minutes. The carrots will lightly steam and cook. Fluff with a fork, taste, and adjust the salt and cinnamon as desired. Add the soaked raisins with their juices and the honey and vanilla to the quinoa and stir.

Serve the porridge in a bowl with a dollop of macadamia nut cream on top. Leftover cream can be stored in an airtight glass container in the refrigerator for up to 5 days.

MACADAMIA NUT CREAM

MAKES ABOUT 1½ CUPS

  1 cup raw macadamia nuts,*
    soaked for at least 2 hours
    Juice of 2 oranges
    Juice of 1 lemon
½ cup filtered water
  1 teaspoon pure vanilla extract
  1 tablespoon grated fresh orange zest
  1 tablespoon pure maple syrup
    Pinch of sea salt

In a high-speed blender, combine the nuts, citrus juices, water, vanilla, orange zest, maple syrup, and salt and blend until creamy. Taste and add more salt, if needed.

*Don't have macadamia nuts? Use all cashews, ½ cashews + ½ almonds, or ½ cashews + ½ sunflower seeds for a creamy and more affordable option.

BASIC OATMEAL
PORRIDGE

MEXICAN CHOCOLATE

SAVORY CORN

PROTEIN-RICH PEAR

OATMEAL PORRIDGE, THREE WAYS

EACH RECIPE SERVES 1 ▪ These three, technically four, recipes showcase the variety rolled oats can bring to your kitchen. Savory Corn may be my favorite out of this bunch. The combination of warming cumin with coconut milk, the southwestern-inspired garnishes, and the sweet corn take this porridge to another level—one that can even be enjoyed for lunch or supper.

BASIC OATMEAL PORRIDGE

1 cup nut or seed milk of your choice (see page 45)

½ cup rolled oats

Pinch of sea salt

SAVORY CORN

1 cup light coconut milk

½ cup rolled oats

Pinch of sea salt

⅔ cup fresh or frozen corn kernels

1 tablespoon honey

½ teaspoon ground cumin

Freshly ground black pepper to taste

Garnishes: diced avocado, chopped fresh cilantro leaves, diced red onion, diced tomato, red pepper flakes

PROTEIN-RICH PEAR

1 cup almond milk (see page 45)

½ cup rolled oats

Pinch of sea salt

2 eggs

1 medium pear, cored and diced

½-inch piece fresh ginger, grated

1 tablespoon grated fresh orange zest

1 teaspoon ground cinnamon

½ teaspoon ground cardamom

2 tablespoons freshly squeezed orange juice

1 tablespoon honey

Garnishes: pumpkin seeds, drizzle of honey, dash of cardamom

MEXICAN CHOCOLATE

1 cup almond milk (see page 45)

½ cup rolled oats

Pinch of sea salt

2 tablespoons chopped pistachios

2 tablespoons pure maple syrup

1 tablespoon tahini

1 tablespoon cocoa powder

Dash of cayenne pepper, or to taste

Dash of ground cinnamon

Garnishes: cacao nibs, drizzle of tahini

In a medium saucepan, combine the nut milk, oats, and salt, plus all the ingredients for the porridge flavor of your choice (but not the garnishes). Bring to a simmer over medium heat, stirring well to combine. Simmer for 20 minutes, stirring continually and scraping down the sides of the pan, until tender. The oats should be dense and the milk absorbed. Serve hot and enjoy with garnishes as desired. Store leftovers in an airtight glass container in the refrigerator for up to 3 days.

SNACKS AND STARTERS

SNACKS:
SMALL BITES TO KEEP YOU ENERGIZED

Snacks are the small bites that tide you over between meals, to be grabbed, gobbled, and savored in the moment no matter where you are. Most of these snacks contain a balanced combination of healthful fats, proteins, vegetables, and fiber to keep you feeling fueled and energized throughout the day. Sweet, salty, crunchy, savory, spicy, chewy, or refreshing and light, these snacks have got you covered! From my staple snacks, like The Only Hummus You'll Ever Need (page 137) and Avocado Toast, Six Ways (page 128), to special bites, like the Bhel Puri (page 122), these are bound to give you a little afternoon jolt of energy.

ULTIMATE ENERGY SEED TRUFFLES

SERVES 12 ▪ Crunchy, sticky, sweet, nutty, and salty—these energy truffles have earned their title for providing energy while being the ultimate seed truffle. Seeds are often overlooked when it comes to standard American diets and it's unfortunate, since they're a powerhouse of minerals and micronutrients, which we're often deficient in thanks to our stressful lives. These truffles are a simple way to give your cells a mineral boost, and the combination of good carbohydrates, healthful fats, and protein gives you sustaining energy. I'll typically make a batch or two of this recipe on my batch-cooking day, freeze half for later, and store the other half in my refrigerator for a quick bite.

2 cups chopped pitted Medjool dates (about 18; see Tip)

3 tablespoons cashew or almond butter (see page 43)

½ cup rolled oats

½ cup raw sunflower seeds

½ cup raw pumpkin seeds

½ cup raw almonds, coarsely chopped

1 tablespoon pure maple syrup

1½ teaspoons pure vanilla extract

Dash of ground cinnamon

Pinch of sea salt

¼ cup coating: hemp seeds, cacao nibs, goji berries, açaí powder, or unsweetened shredded coconut

In a food processor, combine the dates, cashew butter, oats, sunflower and pumpkin seeds, almonds, maple syrup, vanilla, cinnamon, and salt and pulse until the mixture comes together. This mixture will be extremely sticky, so I recommend greasing your hands with coconut oil before handling it.

Take about 1 tablespoon of the mixture and roll into small balls. Spread the coating on a plate and roll each ball until coated. Put the energy balls on a baking sheet in the refrigerator to chill for about 1 hour. Store in an airtight glass container in the refrigerator for up to 2 weeks and enjoy chilled or, if preferred, bring back to room temperature.

Tip: If your dates are on the dry side, soak them in a small bowl of boiling water for 3 minutes before using.

THE BEST CHOCOLATE GRANOLA

MAKES 8 CUPS • Whether it's on top of Coconut Milk Yogurt (page 105) or Oatmeal Porridge, Three Ways (page 115), or a quick on-the-go snack, there's just nothing like homemade granola. The secret to crunchy granola is the combination of good fat and sweeteners, yet most store-bought granolas contain extra oils and refined sugars. Because I prefer granola that's lower in sugar and less sweet, I use coconut oil combined with natural sugars found in rich maple syrup and honey. I have a hunch you'll find yourself grabbing a handful of this chocolate granola and popping back chunk after delicious chunk! Don't say I didn't warn you. . . .

3 cups rolled oats

⅓ cup hemp seeds

1 cup coarsely chopped raw hazelnuts

1 cup coarsely chopped raw walnuts

1 cup raw pumpkin seeds

½ cup pure maple syrup

½ cup coconut oil

⅔ cup cocoa powder

1 teaspoon pure vanilla extract

1 teaspoon sea salt

Dash of ground cinnamon

1 tablespoon cooled espresso

⅓ cup cacao nibs

Tip: Allowing the granola to completely cool before storing or serving is the key to making the granola crunchy.

Preheat the oven to 350°F. Line two baking sheets with parchment paper.

In a large bowl, combine the oats, hemp seeds, hazelnuts, walnuts, and pumpkin seeds and set aside.

In a small saucepan, whisk together the maple syrup, oil, cocoa, vanilla, salt, cinnamon, and cooled espresso. Heat over low heat until the oil is melted, then pour over the oat mixture and stir to coat.

Pour the granola onto the baking sheets and evenly spread with a spatula into a thin layer, being careful not to pack it too firmly onto the sheet, to ensure that your granola comes out crunchy.

Bake for 15 minutes, checking halfway through baking to mix again and respread on the baking sheet. Continue baking for an additional 10 to 15 minutes, until the granola has turned a darker shade of brown. Taste the granola for doneness. The nuts should taste lightly toasted. Remove from the oven and let cool at room temperature. Add in cacao nibs, then store in an airtight glass jar at room temperature for 7 to 10 days.

BHEL PURI (INDIAN STREET FOOD)

SERVES 6 • If you've never had *bhel puri*, it's the ultimate snack and street food in India—it hits the spot on all snacking fronts. Sweet, savory, salty, crunchy, refreshing, spicy, tangy, and creamy all at once, it's an instant crowd-pleaser! Each of the dairy-free, whole-food chutneys and the coconut cream in this recipe take less than 10 minutes to whip together. Get ready to have a mouthful of flavor—and get your hands a little messy.

2 cups puffed rice*

1 cup popped popcorn (see page 50)

1 large apple of your choice, cored and diced

1 cup diced fresh tomatoes

⅓ cup diced red onion

1 teaspoon ground cumin

1 teaspoon chaat masala*

1 teaspoon chili powder

3 tablespoons chopped cashews, toasted (see page 42)

Juice of 1 lemon

Sea salt and freshly ground black pepper

Condiments: Mint-Cilantro Chutney, Tamarind-Date Chutney, Tangy Coconut Cream (recipes follow)

¼ cup chopped fresh cilantro

½ cup sev*

*Find puffed rice in regular grocery stores, but look for chaat masala *spice blend and* sev *at a local Indian market, natural foods store, or international market. Sev is a gluten-free crunchy noodle made from chickpea flour.*

In a large bowl, combine the puffed rice, popcorn, apple, tomatoes, onion, cumin, *chaat masala*, chili powder, cashews, lemon juice, and salt and pepper to taste and set aside. Do not mix until you're ready to serve.

Prepare the condiments just before serving.

Serve the *bhel puri* in small bowls (or in paper cones for the true street food effect), top with the cilantro and *sev*, then drizzle 3 to 4 teaspoons each of the mint-cilantro chutney, the tamarind-date chutney, and the coconut cream. Enjoy immediately.

Tip: Try the leftovers of the condiments as a dipping sauce, marinade, or my favorite way: slathered on top of warm grains like quinoa or millet topped with an egg fried in coconut oil.

(recipe continues)

(recipe continued from page 122)

MINT-CILANTRO CHUTNEY

MAKES ABOUT 1½ CUPS

1 cup chopped fresh mint

1 cup chopped fresh cilantro

1 green chile (seeded if milder chutney is desired)

½-inch piece ginger, peeled and minced

1 clove garlic, minced

1 teaspoon ground cumin

1 teaspoon ground sumac

Juice of 1 lime

Pinch of sea salt

Freshly ground black pepper

In a high-speed blender, combine the mint, cilantro, chile, ginger, garlic, cumin, sumac, lime juice, ⅓ cup water, salt, and pepper to taste and blend until smooth. If the chutney is too thick, add more lime juice or 1 tablespoon of water to thin. Store in an airtight glass container in the refrigerator for up to 1 week.

TANGY COCONUT CREAM

MAKES ABOUT 1½ CUPS

1 (13.5-ounce) can full-fat coconut milk

Juice of 2 lemons

Pinch of sea salt

In a high-speed blender, combine the coconut milk, lemon juice, and salt and blend until smooth. Store in an airtight glass container in the refrigerator for up to 1 week.

TAMARIND-DATE CHUTNEY

MAKES ABOUT ½ CUP

4 tablespoons tamarind paste*
½ cup pitted Medjool dates (4 to 5)
2 tablespoons pure maple syrup
½ teaspoon ground coriander
½ teaspoon ground cumin
½-inch piece ginger, peeled and minced
1 dried red chile (1 inch long), seeded
Pinch of sea salt
Freshly ground black pepper

In a high-speed blender, combine the tamarind paste, dates, maple syrup, coriander, cumin, ginger, chile, salt, and pepper to taste and blend until smooth. This chutney is supposed to be very sweet, but adjust any spices to balance the flavors to your liking. Depending on how fresh your dates are, you may need to add water, 1 tablespoon at a time, to gradually thin the texture, up to 2 tablespoons total. Store in an airtight glass container in the refrigerator for up to 1 week.

*Look for tamarind paste at a local Indian market, natural foods store, or international market.

LACINATO KALE CHIPS, THREE WAYS

SERVES 20+ ▪ You might be thinking a couple things: (1) Kale is so last season, or (2) who eats kale? My mission with this recipe is to completely change your opinion of kale! If I crave anything besides chocolate, it's something crunchy and salty. These kale chips always satisfy my craving and keep me feeling full and great afterward. Nutritional yeast creates a cheesy flavor while effortlessly boosting the protein content. Simple olive oil mixed with dried herbs makes a savory herb variation; lastly, the smoked variation is reminiscent of classic BBQ. Enjoy these on the go or as a topping on a salad, soup, or sandwich!

BASIC KALE CHIPS

5 cups chopped lacinato kale (about 12 leaves), destemmed

¼ cup olive oil

Sea salt and freshly ground black pepper

CHEESY SEASONING

½ cup nutritional yeast

2 tablespoons Dijon mustard

¼ teaspoon garlic powder

Dash of cayenne pepper

HERB SEASONING

½ cup fresh parsley, chopped

½ cup fresh mint leaves, chopped

½ cup fresh chives, chopped

SMOKED SEASONING

½ teaspoon freshly grated nutmeg

½ teaspoon ground cumin

1½ teaspoons smoked paprika

Using an oven: Preheat the oven to 200°F or your lowest oven setting. In a large bowl, toss the chopped kale with the olive oil and the desired seasoning mix. Sprinkle with salt and pepper to taste. Arrange the leaves in a single layer on three baking sheets. Bake for 30 minutes, or until crisp. Transfer the leaves to a rack to cool.

Using a dehydrator: In a large bowl, toss the chopped kale with the olive oil and desired seasonings. Sprinkle with salt and pepper to taste. Arrange the leaves in a single layer on three silicone sheets. Dehydrate at 118°F for 8 hours or overnight until crisp. Flip halfway, or if dehydrating overnight, flip first thing in the morning. Store in an airtight container at room temperature.

AVOCADO TOAST, SIX WAYS

EACH RECIPE SERVES 1 ▪ Avocado toast has taken avocado lovers by storm, and for good reason. The healthful fats found in avocado, coupled with vitamins C, K, E, and B$_6$, and minerals such as potassium, copper, manganese, and magnesium, make this an excellent alternative to butter. Discover which one of these six options will become your new favorite version of a classic snack.

¼ to ½ medium avocado

1 slice gluten-free bread or Artisan Seeded Bread (page 134), toasted

SPINACH PESTO

1 tablespoon Spinach-Basil Pesto (recipe follows)

Pine nuts (optional), toasted (see page 42)

HONEY SEA SALT

1 teaspoon honey

Pinch of sea salt

TOMATO AND SPROUTS

1 tomato, thinly sliced

Handful of fresh sprouts of your choice, such as alfalfa, broccoli, or mixed seed

Pinch each of sea salt and freshly ground black pepper

SUMAC AND SLICED RADISH

1 radish, thinly sliced

Pinch of sea salt

Juice of ½ lemon

Pinch of ground sumac

BLACK GARLIC

1 clove black garlic

Honey

Sea salt

Olive-Chia Caviar (recipe follows)

Mash the avocado flesh onto a piece of toast with the back of a fork, mashing until smooth and creamy. Then follow the instructions below for the variation of your choice.

For the pesto: Make the pesto according to the recipe directions. Spread about 1 tablespoon of the basil pesto on top of the avocado toast, and garnish with toasted pine nuts, if desired.

For the honey sea salt: Drizzle the avocado with the honey and sprinkle with sea salt. Adjust seasoning to taste.

For the tomato and sprouts: Top the avocado with the tomato and sprouts. Sprinkle with sea salt and black pepper to taste.

For the sumac and sliced radish: Top the avocado with the radish, and sprinkle with the salt, lemon juice, and ground sumac.

(recipe continues)

(recipe continued from page 128)

For the black garlic: Mash the black garlic on top of the avocado toast, drizzle with honey, and sprinkle on a pinch of sea salt to taste.

For the olive-chia caviar: Top the avocado with the caviar spread.

SPINACH-BASIL PESTO

MAKES 1½ CUPS ▪ *Use as a spread on pasta, warm grains, and sandwiches; serve as a vegetable dip; or dollop on eggs.*

2 cups fresh basil leaves
2 cups chopped fresh spinach
½ cup olive oil
1 cup walnuts, finely chopped
½ cup nutritional yeast
1 tablespoon hemp seeds
1 teaspoon sea salt
Freshly ground black pepper

In a high-speed blender, combine the basil, spinach, oil, walnuts, nutritional yeast, hemp seeds, salt, and pepper to taste and blend until smooth. Adjust seasonings to taste and add more olive oil to thin depending on your desired texture. Store in an airtight glass container in the refrigerator for 1 week.

OLIVE-CHIA CAVIAR

MAKES ½ CUP

¼ cup chia seeds
½ cup filtered water
3 tablespoons chopped pitted olives
Honey (optional)

Soak the chia seeds in the water until gelatinized, about 30 minutes, then stir in the chopped olives. If too salty, add a touch of honey. Store caviar leftovers in an airtight glass container in the refrigerator for 1 week. Use as a spread on pasta, warm grains, and sandwiches; serve as a vegetable dip; or dollop on eggs.

TURMERIC AEBLESKIVERS WITH MANGO JAM

MAKES 20 AEBLESKIVERS OR 24 MINI-MUFFINS • Aebleskivers (EH-bleh-skeevors) are a traditional Danish breakfast and snack food typically made with flour, eggs, water, cream, sugar, and salt and eaten with sweet jams such as blackberry, black currant, raspberry, or strawberry. They're basically a delicious and fluffy bite-size puff pancake dipped in sweet jam—*this* is globally delicious. You can enjoy these with delicious homemade mango jam or dusted with a powdered-sugar topping. You can also achieve the bite-size concept with a mini-muffin tin.

2 cups gluten-free all-purpose flour

1 teaspoon sea salt

½ teaspoon ground cinnamon

2 teaspoons ground turmeric

3 eggs, separated

2 cups almond milk (see page 45)

2 tablespoons freshly squeezed lemon juice

4 teaspoons raw apple cider vinegar

Mango Jam (recipe follows)

Turmeric Powdered Coconut Sugar (optional; recipe follows)

In a large bowl, combine the flour, salt, cinnamon, and turmeric. In a small bowl, whisk together the egg yolks, almond milk, lemon juice, and vinegar. Add this mixture to the flour mixture and stir until combined.

Using an electric mixer on medium speed, beat the egg whites until fluffy and soft peaks form, about 3 minutes. Using a large rubber spatula, fold the egg whites with a wide and gentle sweeping motion into the batter; the goal is to have a light and fluffy batter.

Using an aebleskiver pan: Heavily grease the aebleskiver pan with coconut oil; you'll do this in between the batches. Heat the pan over medium heat. When hot, fill each cup about two-thirds full with the batter and cook for 1 to 2 minutes. The outside of the aebleskiver will be brown and the top will have bubbles, which is the sign they are ready to turn. Loosen the aebleskivers by running a table knife around the outside of each one and lifting up slightly to loosen it from the bottom. Turn with a fork. Cook for another

(recipe continues)

(recipe continued from page 131)

minute, or until tender and the batter on the inside is cooked through. Repeat this process until all the batter has been used.

Using a mini-muffin tin: Preheat the oven to 350°F. Grease 24 cups of a mini-muffin tin with coconut oil. Pour the batter to two-thirds full and bake for 10 minutes, or until fluffy and golden brown. Serve the aebleskivers warm with the mango jam on the side. Or dust with a touch of the turmeric coconut sugar, if desired.

MANGO JAM

MAKES ABOUT 1 CUP

½ cup filtered water
2 small ripe mangoes, peeled and chopped (about 2 cups)
1 tablespoon honey
1 orange, zested and juiced
3 tablespoons ground chia seeds (see Note)
½ teaspoon sea salt

In a small saucepan, combine the water and mangoes and bring to a boil. Reduce to a simmer and add the honey, orange juice, chia seeds, and salt. Stir to combine and cook over low heat for 10 to 15 minutes, until thick. Add 1 tablespoon of the orange zest and let cool to room temperature.

Note: White chia seeds will keep the mango jam a yellow color. If you use black chia seeds, the jam will be brown (but still just as delicious).

TURMERIC POWDERED COCONUT SUGAR

MAKES ¼ CUP

⅓ cup coconut sugar
¼ teaspoon ground cinnamon
¼ teaspoon ground turmeric

In a nut/seed grinder or high-speed blender, combine the ingredients and process until the sugar has broken down into a powder.

ARTISAN SEEDED BREAD

MAKES 4 ROUND LOAVES • There's something about breaking bread with others around the table: the sense of camaraderie and community, of enjoying the present moment around good food. In this, bread is so much more than just what we put in our mouths. This seeded loaf is the ultimate gluten-free, crunchy, hearty accompaniment for any number of meals, including a piping-hot bowl of chili or soup, velvety poached eggs, or salads. And, of course, it can simply be eaten plain, in all its glory. You can easily cut this recipe in half or freeze the extra loaves for later (see Tip).

6½ cups gluten-free all-purpose flour

½ cup buckwheat flour

2 tablespoons ground flaxseeds

2 tablespoons hemp seeds

2 tablespoons poppy seeds, plus more for topping

2 tablespoons chia seeds

¾ cup raw sunflower seeds

¼ cup sesame seeds

¼ cup raw pumpkin seeds

1 tablespoon sea salt

¼ cup honey

4½ cups warm water (105°F)

1 tablespoon active dry yeast

3 eggs

In a large bowl, whisk together the flours, ground flaxseeds, hemp seeds, poppy seeds, chia seeds, sunflower seeds, sesame seeds, pumpkin seeds, and salt.

In a small bowl, stir together the honey and warm water until the honey has dissolved. Add the yeast and let rest for 5 minutes to activate. Mix in the eggs with a fork. Pour this wet mixture into the flour-seed mixture and stir with a spoon until combined. Let this dough sit at room temperature loosely covered with plastic wrap until the dough rises, 2 hours.

After the dough has risen, refrigerate covered for 2 hours. Place a large handful of the chilled dough (one-quarter of the mixture) on a parchment-lined cutting board. Using wet hands, create a large dough ball and smooth with your fingers. Repeat with the remaining dough. (If you prefer to make just one loaf now, see Tip for storing the remaining dough.) Cover the dough balls with plastic wrap and let them rest at room temperature for at least 1 hour.

Preheat the oven to 450°F.

(recipe continues)

(recipe continued from page 134)

Once the bread has rested, place a pizza stone (for crispiest crust) or baking sheet in the oven to heat for at least 15 minutes before baking the bread. Cut an X at the top of the loaf before placing the dough onto the hot pizza stone.

Pour 1 cup water into a baking pan and place the pan on the lowest rack of the oven. Immediately shut the oven door and bake for 50 to 60 minutes, until browned and firm. You want the bread to be crisp and hard on the outside and soft and moist on the inside. Poke a knife or toothpick into the loaf to check for moisture and softness inside.

Let cool completely on a wire rack before cutting into sandwich slices, or enjoy warm by tearing apart with your hands.

Tip: If 4 loaves are too many, you can always halve the recipe. You can also refrigerate the unbaked dough for up to 1 week, to bake at a later time. I prefer to make the full recipe, however, and freeze a couple loaves for later use. Slice the bread before freezing, thaw overnight in the refrigerator, and toast to enjoy it after thawing. You may also freeze the unbaked dough. Just thaw before baking and continue with the baking steps.

THE ONLY HUMMUS YOU'LL EVER NEED

SERVES 6 • Whether you want a quick snack for yourself or for guests coming over, this hummus is an indispensable recipe. It's a delicious creamy dip or spread containing both protein and fiber. The base recipe is delicious on its own, but have fun adding ingredients to switch up the flavor. The possibilities are endless.

2 cups cooked chickpeas or 1 (15-ounce) can, drained and rinsed

3 heaping tablespoons tahini

2 heaping tablespoons olive oil

2 cloves garlic

Juice of 2 lemons

2 tablespoons filtered water

1 teaspoon sea salt

Pinch of cayenne pepper

Pinch of freshly grated nutmeg

Freshly ground black pepper

OPTIONAL ADD-INS (CHOOSE ONE)

¼ cup sun-dried tomatoes

⅓ cup pitted olives

1 cup cut-up fruit, such as mango, peaches, or pear

½ cup roasted red bell pepper

2 tablespoons sliced jalapeños

1 tablespoon curry powder

½ cup pureed roasted beets

1 cup pureed cooked carrots

In a high-speed blender, combine the chickpeas, tahini, olive oil, garlic, lemon juice, water, salt, cayenne, nutmeg, black pepper to taste, and an optional add-in of choice, if desired. Blend until smooth. Adjust seasonings to taste. Store in an airtight glass container in the refrigerator for up to 1 week.

Tip: Use hummus as a dip with bite-size portions of raw vegetables and fruits or gluten-free crackers, or slathered as a spread on Artisan Seeded Bread (page 134). Or to turn it into a salad dressing, combine a couple of tablespoons of hummus with a couple of tablespoons of raw apple cider vinegar and olive oil—it's super creamy and delicious!

THE BEST GUACAMOLE EVER

SERVES 4 • Guacamole has a bad reputation for being calorie heavy—but it's also nutrient dense, which is why you can always find it in my refrigerator. This guacamole recipe is loaded with healthful fats, vitamins, minerals, and fiber, and tastes darn good on almost everything!

What defines the *best* guacamole for me is one that covers all the bases: It's creamy, crunchy, spicy, tangy, and . . . addicting. Try the classic as a spread on sandwich bread or dolloped onto salad greens or warm grains. The grapefruit variation is juicy and rich in vitamin C. In another variation, adding green peas is a great way to sneak in extra veggies, protein, and fiber.

2 medium avocados

¼ cup diced red onion

1 jalapeño pepper, diced

2 large cloves garlic, diced

½ cup chopped fresh cilantro

¼ cup diced cherry tomatoes

1 to 2 teaspoons sea salt to taste

1 teaspoon ground cumin

Juice of 1 lemon

Juice of 1 lime

Dash of cayenne pepper, or to taste

Freshly ground black pepper

½ lemon, sliced

In a large bowl, combine the avocados, red onion, jalapeño, garlic, cilantro, tomatoes, salt, cumin, lemon juice, lime juice, cayenne, and black pepper to taste. Mash the avocados with the back of a fork until all the ingredients are combined and you've reached your desired consistency.

Arrange the lemon slices so that they cover the entire top surface of the guacamole. This keeps it fresh and slows down the oxidation. Store guacamole in an airtight glass container in the refrigerator for up to 5 days.

For a pea variation: In a food processor, gently pulse 1 cup thawed frozen peas with the juice of 1 lemon. Stir the mixture into the guacamole and adjust seasonings to taste.

For a grapefruit variation: Roughly chop the segments of 1 grapefruit and gently fold them into the guacamole. Adjust seasonings to taste.

SALADS:
NOT JUST A BOWL
OF LETTUCE LEAVES

A sampling of my favorite, soon to be your favorite, salads: full of nutrients, flavor, fiber, and flexibility. Salads are no longer a supporting cast to entrées; these have been transformed by using fruits, grains, roasted vegetables, and combinations of cold and warm ingredients. You can change it up depending on the time of year and your local fresh ingredients. Salads are a delicious way to enjoy and get excited about vegetables again! Enjoy salads as a starter for a meal, or as an entrée by adding healthful fats and protein-rich ingredients like chickpeas, lentils, or tempeh.

BASIC GREENS WITH LEMON-SUMAC DRESSING

SERVES 2 TO 4 · Everyone needs a simple green salad that they can toss together quickly for an impromptu supper with friends or a meal that's fresh and light. Take this salad to the next level with sunchokes (a.k.a. Jerusalem artichokes). I instantly fell in love with their hearty and meaty texture and their flavor, which is similar to that of artichoke hearts. Citrus is heavenly with sunchokes, and this lemon-sumac dressing is a perfect match. Make this simple green salad into a sophisticated side dish by topping it with popcorn—yes popcorn! It adds an amazing flavor and texture, and brings the whole dish together.

2 cups chopped peeled sunchokes*

4 tablespoons olive oil

½ teaspoon ground sumac

Sea salt and freshly ground black pepper

2 cups coarsely chopped romaine lettuce

2 cups watercress

Juice of 2 lemons

Garnishes: ¼ cup chopped walnuts, lightly toasted (see page 42), per serving; ¼ cup popped popcorn (see page 50), per serving

*If you cannot find sunchokes, use canned or frozen artichoke hearts, which are equally delicious, though less hearty.

Preheat the oven to 350°F. Line a baking sheet with parchment paper.

Evenly spread out the sunchokes on the baking sheet, drizzle with 2 tablespoons of the oil, and sprinkle on the ground sumac and a pinch each of salt and pepper. Bake for 35 to 45 minutes, until tender.

In a large serving bowl, combine the romaine, watercress, and roasted sunchokes and drizzle with the remaining 2 tablespoons oil and the lemon juice. Finish with a pinch each of salt and pepper. Garnish as desired before serving—I can't recommend the popcorn enough!

Nutrition Tip: Sunchokes contain a type of fiber called inulin, which is great for digestion but may cause bloating or gas in some people—just like cruciferous veggies do. Take it easy if you're new to eating them and take a digestive enzyme beforehand (see page 289) to help ease the symptoms. Along with fiber, sunchokes contain iron, potassium, and B vitamins.

BLOOD ORANGE AND GRAPEFRUIT SALAD WITH CINNAMON

SERVES 4 • I naturally gravitate toward warm ingredients during the cooler months of the year, whether warm in temperature or warm in heat-producing qualities. Because this all-raw salad is served at room temperature or cold, I use one of my favorite spices to bring a natural rise in heat within the body: cinnamon. Cinnamon has been shown to help reduce blood sugar spikes and keep our blood sugar levels nice and steady whenever we eat any carbohydrate, such as fruit. The arrangement of thinly sliced citrus fruits makes for an impressive presentation for the many holidays during the fall and winter season.

2 large pink grapefruits

2 blood oranges

¼ cup extra-virgin olive oil

2 tablespoons raw apple cider vinegar

½ teaspoon sea salt

¼ cup chopped fresh sage

Freshly ground black pepper

½ teaspoon ground cinnamon, for dusting

Keep the peel on the fruits to start, which makes slicing them into thin pieces much easier. With a sharp knife, slice the grapefruits and the oranges into thin rounds. Remove the peel from the perimeter of all the rounds. You may do so by using your finger, or make a small slit into the peel and continue to tear the peel off—you'll want to be delicate with this entire process so as not to damage the round shape.

In a small bowl, whisk together the olive oil, vinegar, salt, sage, and pepper to taste.

Arrange the fruit rounds on a large platter or plate, alternating the colors. Drizzle with the vinaigrette and dust with the cinnamon just before serving. Serve immediately or store in an airtight glass container in the refrigerator for 1 day.

MASSAGED BEET, CARROT, AND BRUSSELS SPROUT SALAD WITH CITRUS-TAHINI DRESSING

SERVES 4 • This recipe was inspired by Chef Jonathan Waxman, whom I met at the Music City Food and Wine Festival here in Nashville. This nutrient-dense play on coleslaw combines shaved Brussels sprouts with grated beets and carrots. The vegetables are massaged and mixed with a creamy tahini dressing, and the flavors melt together. I enjoy this most as a leftover, after it's been marinating and sitting in the refrigerator for a couple of days.

CITRUS-TAHINI DRESSING

¼ cup tahini

3 tablespoons filtered water

1 tablespoon raw apple cider vinegar

1 tablespoon olive oil

1 tablespoon pure maple syrup

Juice of 2 lemons

1 clove garlic, minced

Pinch of sea salt

Freshly ground black pepper

SALAD

½ pound Brussels sprouts

½ pound beets (about 4 large)

½ pound medium carrots (about 6 large)

1 cup thinly sliced napa cabbage

¼ cup olive oil

Juice of 3 lemons

Pinch of sea salt

¼ cup pine nuts, lightly toasted (see page 42)

Freshly ground black pepper

For the citrus-tahini dressing: In a high-speed blender, combine the tahini, water, vinegar, oil, maple syrup, lemon juice, garlic, salt, and pepper to taste and blend until smooth.

For the salad: Using a mandoline or a food processor fitted with the slicing blade, carefully run the individual Brussels sprouts through to thinly shave. Using a grater or food processor fitted with the grating blade, grate the beets, carrots, and cabbage. Transfer all the prepared vegetables to a large bowl.

Add the oil, lemon juice, and salt and gently work into the vegetables with your hands in a massaging action. Be sure to apply pressure to break down the leaves of the cabbage and Brussels sprouts. Do this for 5 minutes, or until the vegetables are softened to your desired texture.

Pour the dressing over the vegetables and gently toss to combine and coat. Toss in the toasted pine nuts. Adjust the seasoning with salt and pepper. Serve chilled or at room temperature.

WINTER CITRUS-GRAIN SALAD

SERVES 4 ▪ Who said salad is only for summer? Warm grains in a salad on their own are delicious. Cooking them in vegetable broth or stock instead of water infuses each grain with a boost of flavor. Mineral- and antioxidant-rich watercress; chickpeas; and bright and tangy grapefruit, orange, and green apple all add to this salad's taste and texture. Supersimple, this is a refreshing sticks-to-your-ribs kind of salad.

1 cup red or black quinoa
(see Note)

2 cups vegetable stock

2 cups watercress

2 tablespoons olive oil

2 tablespoons sherry vinegar

Juice of 2 lemons

2 teaspoons ground sumac

1 teaspoon sea salt

Freshly ground black pepper

¼ cup hemp seeds

1 large navel orange, peeled and segmented

1 large grapefruit, peeled and segmented

½ cup pomegranate seeds

1 green apple, diced

2 cups cooked chickpeas or 1 (15-ounce) can, drained and rinsed

Cook the quinoa according to the how-to on page 39, substituting the vegetable stock for the water. Let cool to room temperature before continuing to the next step if you'd like your salad served at room temperature; otherwise continue with the next step using hot quinoa.

In a large bowl, combine the watercress, oil, vinegar, lemon juice, sumac, salt, and pepper to taste and gently toss to combine. Add the quinoa, hemp seeds, citrus segments, pomegranate seeds, apple, and chickpeas and toss gently until everything is evenly distributed. Serve as is, or turn into an entrée by adding your favorite protein choices or healthful fats. Store in an airtight glass container in the refrigerator for up to 1 week.

Note: You may use white quinoa as well as black or red. Red and black varieties are heartier and tend to hold up better with dressing and for leftovers the next day.

MELON, FENNEL, AND ASPARAGUS SHAVED SALAD

SERVES 4 ▪ Eating whole foods is wonderful, but eating the same whole foods time and time again can become, well, boring. As soon as I feel that sense of mundane with a meal, I immediately switch up the ingredients, combine them in new ways, and play with textures. The way we perceive a food, visually or conceptually, greatly affects how we'll enjoy it—especially if a food's novelty has worn off. Shaving the asparagus, fennel, and melon makes a world of difference and gives this salad an undeniably soft, delicate, juicy yet crunchy texture. And save your fennel fronds: They're flavorful additions to salads and sandwiches, and fennel has been used for centuries for its ability to help digestion.

1½ pounds honeydew melon

1 fennel bulb

12 large asparagus spears (about 1 pound), trimmed and peeled

2 tablespoons olive oil, plus more for drizzling

1 teaspoon grated fresh orange zest

Juice of 1 orange

Juice of 1 lemon

¼ cup chopped fresh mint

¼ cup chopped pitted green olives

Pinch of sea salt

Freshly ground black pepper

2 tablespoons pine nuts, toasted (see page 42)

Remove the rind and seeds from the honeydew and cut the melon lengthwise into strips. Remove the fennel stalks and fronds. Chop 2 tablespoons of the fronds and reserve. Using a mandoline, shave the fennel bulb and place in a large bowl, then add the fennel fronds. Use a vegetable peeler to peel the asparagus spears and honeydew melon into thin ribbons. Place in the bowl with the fennel.

Add the oil, orange zest, orange juice, lemon juice, mint, olives, salt, and pepper to taste to the bowl and mix to evenly coat. Taste for seasoning and adjust the salt and pepper accordingly. Top with the toasted pine nuts and a drizzle of olive oil, and serve at room temperature or chilled. This salad is best served immediately, but it may be stored in an airtight glass container in the refrigerator for up to 3 days.

Nutrition Tip: Asparagus is a natural diuretic and a nutrient powerhouse containing vitamins K, C, E, and A; B vitamins; and minerals such as copper, selenium, manganese, phosphorus, potassium, choline, zinc, iron, magnesium, and calcium.

SLICED RADISH AND APPLE SALAD

SERVES 4 TO 6 • I first tried this recipe on willing and excited guests during my Fall Supper Club, making use of fresh radishes and fall apples from Bloomsbury Farms here in Nashville. Even feeding fifty guests, it took less than 10 minutes to prepare! Radishes are either wildly loved or avoided owing to their bold and zesty flavor. As an active member of the radish fan club, I adore using them in any dish that needs a little crunch and personality. When they are thinly sliced and layered alongside sweet apples, their flavor truly shines and a beautiful flavor marriage ensues.

4 large radishes

2 large green apples

1 large Fuji apple

¼ cup extra-virgin olive oil

2 tablespoons sherry vinegar

1 tablespoon grated fresh lemon zest

Juice of 1 lemon

1 tablespoon pure maple syrup

Pinch of sea salt

Freshly ground black pepper

Garnishes: thinly sliced fresh mint; olive oil; ¼ cup chopped hazelnuts, toasted (see page 42)

Using a mandoline or knife, thinly slice all the radishes and apples to about a ¼-inch thickness. Place the sliced radishes and apples in a large shallow salad bowl. I enjoy alternating the layers of radish and apple; it makes for beautiful presentation and flavor. Drizzle with the oil, vinegar, lemon zest, lemon juice, maple syrup, salt, and pepper to taste and toss. Adjust seasonings to taste.

Garnish with the mint, oil, and hazelnuts. Serve immediately. Leftovers may be stored in an airtight glass container in the refrigerator for 2 days.

Nutrition Tip: Radishes contain great amounts of vitamin C and are digestion friendly owing to their fiber content. They also contain antifungal and antibacterial properties as well as antioxidants called indoles, which support our bodies' detoxification.

MOROCCAN MILLET SALAD

SERVES 4 · Though I've never been to Morocco, whenever I make this dish, I feel it totally transports me there. This salad celebrates bold flavors, seasonal and local ingredients, and a marriage of sweet and salty. It can easily be thrown together in under 25 minutes and the millet soaks up the dressing like a little sponge. What's even better is that the flavor only improves after it sits in the refrigerator overnight! Enjoy this salad on its own, rolled inside lettuce wraps, or sandwiched in between portobello mushroom caps.

1 cup millet

2 cups vegetable stock

⅓ cup chopped pitted green olives

2 cloves garlic, minced

1 shallot, thinly sliced

½ cup sun-dried tomatoes

Juice of 1 lemon

2 tablespoons capers, drained and rinsed

⅓ cup chopped pitted Medjool dates (about 3)

2 tablespoons grapeseed oil

2 tablespoons Dijon mustard

2 tablespoons raw apple cider vinegar

Pinch of sea salt

Freshly ground black pepper

¼ cup chopped fresh mint

¼ cup chopped fresh parsley

Garnishes: ½ cup pine nuts, toasted (see page 42); chopped fresh mint; olive oil; freshly squeezed lemon juice

In a large dry skillet, gently toast the millet over medium heat for 5 minutes, or until golden brown. Watch carefully so the millet doesn't burn.

In a large saucepan, bring the vegetable stock to a boil, add the toasted millet, reduce the heat to medium-low, cover, and cook for 15 minutes. Remove from the heat, let sit for 10 minutes covered, then remove the lid and fluff with a fork.

In a small bowl, combine the olives, garlic, shallot, sun-dried tomatoes, lemon juice, capers, dates, grapeseed oil, Dijon mustard, vinegar, salt, and pepper to taste. Pour this dressing on top of the fluffed millet. Add the mint and parsley and stir. Garnish before serving warm. Store leftovers in an airtight glass container in the refrigerator for up to 4 days.

Nutrition Tip: Dates are a great source of potassium, carbohydrates (simple sugars for quick energy), manganese, magnesium, copper, and other trace minerals.

SOUPS:
A HUG FOR YOUR STOMACH

With just one bowl, soup has the power to transform your mood, bring back childhood memories, create a cozy atmosphere and fragrance in your home, bring some comfort to a friend in need, or simply nourish your body and soul. Soup is incredibly versatile: It can be served as a hearty entrée, a side dish, or a start to any meal. I encourage you to make each soup your own, as they are incredibly forgiving—adjust your seasonings to taste and add to the pot what you love (and keep out what you don't). Whether it's a stock-based soup like the Turmeric Lemon Broth with Corona Beans (page 158) or a hearty stew like the Chocolate-Cinnamon-Walnut Chili (page 161), all these soups have their purpose, time, and place to soothe. These recipes can be made in large batches to feed a hungry family, but if you're just feeding one or two, you'll be grateful to have plenty of leftovers to freeze for later.

TURMERIC LEMON BROTH WITH CORONA BEANS

SERVES 6 TO 8 • This is the soup you want on your bedside or couch when your body is craving something warming and, dare I say, healing. The combination of anti-inflammatory-rich turmeric with refreshing vitamin C–rich lemons in a gorgeous broth . . . is nourishing on so many levels. During the winter, I love adding roasted chestnuts for added bite.

2 cups dried corona beans*

2 tablespoons coconut oil

1 sweet onion, chopped

3 cloves garlic, minced

1 small bunch of chives, sliced diagonally

1 teaspoon red pepper flakes

Pinch of sea salt

Freshly ground black pepper

2 cups vegetable stock

2 cups filtered water

3 tablespoons white miso

2 lemons, thinly sliced

1-inch fresh turmeric, peeled and grated

1 pound fresh chestnuts,* roasted (optional; see "Roasting Chestnuts," opposite)

Juice of 3 lemons

Garnishes: additional chopped chives, a dollop of Cashew Cheese (page 49), a dash of red pepper flakes, chopped fresh mint and/or cilantro, drizzle of olive oil, honey

Cook the beans until tender following the how-to for cooking beans and legumes on page 41.

In a large soup pot, warm the oil over medium heat, then add the onion, garlic, chives, red pepper flakes, salt, and black pepper to taste. Stir occasionally until the onion has softened, about 8 minutes. Add the stock, water, miso, lemon slices, turmeric, cooked corona beans, and chestnuts (if using). Add the lemon juice and adjust seasonings to taste. Bring the mixture to a simmer and cook for 20 minutes. Garnish as desired and serve hot.

Leftover soup may be stored in an airtight glass container in the refrigerator for 4 to 6 days or in the freezer for up to 2 weeks.

*Corona beans are also called gigante beans, so either may be used. If you don't have corona beans, try lima or kidney beans instead. If you don't have access to fresh chestnuts, you may substitute canned or frozen chestnuts. Just rinse them well before adding to the soup.

ROASTING CHESTNUTS
Preheat the oven to 400°F.

Score an X into the hard shell of each chestnut using a sharp paring knife. This helps release the moisture and makes the peeling process much easier. Evenly spread the scored chestnuts on a baking sheet, lightly drizzle with olive oil and roast for about 45 minutes, or until tender. Allow the cooked chestnuts to cool enough for you to handle them. Using your fingers, peel and discard the outer shells.

CHOCOLATE-CINNAMON-WALNUT CHILI

SERVES 8 TO 10 • Born and raised in Cincinnati, Ohio, I take my chili very seriously. Anytime I make this chili for my friends here in Nashville, they immediately say, "This is amazing. What's in here?" The subtle rich dark chocolate and warming cinnamon take this chili to a whole new level of comfort. When I was growing up, my mother would let chili slowly cook all day long to where it was perfectly flavored and reduced to a thick consistency just in time for supper. Very purposeful, very special, and damn good.

2 tablespoons olive oil

1 medium red onion, diced

3 cloves garlic, minced

2 jalapeño peppers, seeded and sliced

1 to 1½ tablespoons ground cinnamon, to taste

1 to 1½ tablespoons ground cumin, to taste

½ tablespoon smoked paprika

1 teaspoon sea salt

Freshly ground black pepper

2 cups diced fresh tomatoes or 1 (15-ounce) can

2 cups tomato sauce or 1 (15-ounce) can

2 cups vegetable stock

1 cup cooked brown lentils

1 cup cooked kidney beans or about ½ (15-ounce) can, drained and rinsed

1 cup cooked butter beans or Great Northern beans or about ½ (15-ounce) can, drained and rinsed

1 cup raw walnuts, lightly toasted (see page 42)

3 ounces dark chocolate

2 cinnamon sticks

Garnishes: diced sweet onion, dash of ground cinnamon, fresh cilantro leaves, hot sauce, crushed walnuts

In a large soup pot, warm the oil over medium heat. Add the onion and garlic and cook until softened, about 5 minutes. Add the jalapeños, ground cinnamon, cumin, smoked paprika, salt, and pepper to taste and cook for another 2 to 3 minutes so the spices become fragrant.

Add the tomatoes, tomato sauce, stock, lentils, kidney beans, butter beans, walnuts, chocolate, and cinnamon sticks. Taste test while simmering; take out the cinnamon sticks when the desired flavor is reached or leave in for the full cooking time. Simmer over medium-low heat for 4 hours or more, until thickened. You may adjust the cook time depending on how thick you like your chili. If you prefer it on the thin side, add more stock. Before serving, pick out the cinnamon sticks and adjust seasonings to your taste.

Serve the chili over gluten-free pasta for a true Cincinnati flare. Top with garnishes. Store in an airtight glass container for up to 1 week in the refrigerator or freeze for 2 to 3 weeks.

MOROCCAN TOMATO-CHICKPEA STEW WITH WALNUT GREMOLATA

SERVES 12 • This vegetarian stew has had many carnivores saying, "I can't believe this is healthful and meatless!" I love the use of warming, hearty flavors in Moroccan cooking. *Ras el hanout* translates as "the king of the shop" and is my favorite Moroccan spice blend for adding a punch of flavor.

2 tablespoons coconut oil

1 large red onion, chopped

1 tablespoon sea salt

1 teaspoon freshly ground black pepper

2 large zucchini, chopped

3 cloves garlic, minced

1-inch piece fresh ginger, peeled and minced

2 teaspoons ground turmeric

2 teaspoons ground coriander

1 tablespoon ras el hanout

2 teaspoons ground cumin

1 teaspoon cayenne pepper

9 tablespoons tomato paste

3 cups vegetable stock

2 cups diced fresh tomatoes or 1 (15-ounce) can

2 cups tomato sauce or 1 (15-ounce) can

4 cups cooked chickpeas or 2 (15-ounce) cans, drained and rinsed

Walnut Gremolata (recipe follows)

In a large Dutch oven, melt the coconut oil over medium-high heat. Add the onion, salt, and pepper. Cook for 5 minutes, stirring occasionally, until the onion has softened.

Add the zucchini, garlic, ginger, turmeric, coriander, *ras el hanout*, cumin, and cayenne and cook for 5 minutes, until the spices are fragrant.

Add the tomato paste, vegetable stock, diced tomatoes, tomato sauce, and chickpeas. Reduce the heat to medium-low and simmer for 1 hour, stirring occasionally, until thick.

Serve the stew in a large bowl and top with 1 to 2 tablespoons of gremolata per serving. Alternatively, you can serve the stew on a bed of cooked quinoa or millet. The stew may be stored in an airtight glass container in the refrigerator for up to 1 week.

(recipe continues)

(recipe continued from page 162)

WALNUT GREMOLATA

MAKES ABOUT 1⅓ CUPS • *Walnut gremolata is a pleasant, bright, and refreshing topping made from chopped nuts, fresh herbs, lemon juice, salt, and garlic. It's a simple topping and condiment that also works well on sandwiches, grains, tacos, and more!*

1 cup chopped raw walnuts, toasted (see page 42)
⅔ cup chopped fresh parsley
¼ to ⅓ cup chopped fresh mint
2 cloves garlic, minced
3 tablespoons walnut oil
2 tablespoons grated fresh lemon zest
  Juice of 2 lemons
1 teaspoon sea salt
  Freshly ground black pepper

In a small bowl, combine the walnuts, parsley, mint, garlic, walnut oil, lemon zest, lemon juice, salt, and pepper to taste and mix with a fork. Store gremolata in an airtight glass container in the refrigerator for up to 2 weeks.

ULTIMATE PHO BOWL WITH DUMPLINGS

SERVES 4 • You know those nights when you're craving a huge bowl of noodles? This recipe is meant to entertain those cravings in a "Vietnamese comfort food meets chicken and dumplings" kind of way. Making gluten-free noodles, for me, is tricky, but rolling dough in a ball and calling it a day is so simple that everyone can do it. I guarantee you'll be a dumpling-making pro after this recipe. Share a pot with your friends and family and start making memories.

SOUP

- 2 tablespoons cold-pressed sesame oil
- 1 large red onion, quartered
- 4-inch piece fresh ginger, peeled and halved
- 2 cinnamon sticks
- 2 star anise
- 4 or 5 cloves garlic, minced
- 1 teaspoon coriander seeds
- 4 cups vegetable stock
- 2 cups filtered water
- ½ cup tamari or nama shoyu
- 1 bunch of scallions (white and light green parts), diagonally sliced
- 4 carrots, coarsely chopped

DUMPLINGS

- 1 cup white rice flour (see page 47)
- 1 cup gluten-free all-purpose flour
- 1 clove garlic, minced
- 1 teaspoon sea salt
- ½ teaspoon freshly ground black pepper
- 1 teaspoon baking powder
- 1 egg, beaten
- ¾ cup almond milk (see page 45)
- 1 tablespoon olive oil

GARNISHES

Protein: baked tofu, shelled edamame

Vegetables: mushrooms of your choice; thinly sliced bok choy, napa cabbage, or broccoli; mung bean sprouts

Thinly sliced red onion or scallions

Sliced chile pepper

Lime wedges

Chopped fresh herbs: cilantro, Thai basil, or mint

Condiments: hoisin sauce, gluten-free soy sauce, or sriracha

For the soup: In a medium skillet, warm the sesame oil over medium heat. Add the onion and ginger and stir about 5 minutes, until the aromatics start to brown. Set aside.

In a large soup pot over medium-low heat, dry-toast the cinnamon sticks, star anise, garlic, and coriander seeds, stirring to prevent burning, about 4 minutes. When the spices are aromatic, add the stock, water, tamari, scallions, carrots, and the browned onion-ginger mixture. Simmer the stock for 1 hour to enrich the flavor.

(recipe continues)

(recipe continued from page 165)

Meanwhile, for the dumplings: In a small bowl, combine the flours, garlic, salt, pepper, and baking powder. In another small bowl, whisk together the egg, almond milk, and olive oil, pour into the flour mixture, and stir to combine. A dough will start to form—if this dough is too wet or sticky, add additional all-purpose flour gradually; be sure not to overwork the dough. Take about ½ tablespoon dough and gently roll into a ball, set aside, and repeat until all the remaining dough is finished; you should have about 10 dumplings, but the yield will vary depending upon how large you make them.

Gently add the dumplings, one at a time, to the simmering broth in the soup pot. Cook until the dumplings float to the top of the soup, about 7 minutes. Do not cook more dumplings than you're going to eat. Leftover soup and dough mixture may be stored separately in airtight glass containers in the refrigerator. When reheating the soup, add the dumplings and cook as above.

To serve, place each garnish in a bowl. You can arrange them in sections, as pictured, or stir together.

ZINGER WARMING SOUP

SERVES 4 TO 6 • This is my go-to soup when I'm feeling under the weather—some people may go for chicken noodle, I go for zinger warming soup. This hot, smooth soup contains a host of nutrients and health benefits in one pot; it's cozy, warming, and hits the spot. The spices used—turmeric, ginger, garlic, black pepper, chile—are all warming spices. The vegetables, aromatics, and spices all contain immune-strengthening nutrients you can enjoy year-round.

2 tablespoons coconut oil, plus more if needed

5 medium stalks celery, chopped

1 medium sweet onion, chopped

Sea salt and freshly ground black pepper

5 cloves garlic, chopped

10 medium carrots, chopped

1 fresh red chile, halved lengthwise

1 tablespoon ground turmeric

2-inch piece fresh ginger, peeled and minced

½ teaspoon ground cinnamon

Dash of cayenne pepper, or to taste

4 cups vegetable stock

Filtered water

1 medium orange, peeled

Juice of 1 lemon

Garnishes: chopped fresh parsley, snipped fresh chives, roasted pumpkin seeds, a drizzle of full-fat coconut milk

In a large soup pot, warm the oil over medium heat. Add the celery, onion, and salt and black pepper to taste. Cook for 5 minutes. Add the garlic and continue to cook over medium-low heat for 8 to 10 minutes, until the onion is translucent and the celery softens.

If the pan looks dry, add another tablespoon of oil. Add the carrots, chile, turmeric, ginger, cinnamon, cayenne, stock, and enough water to cover. Bring this mixture to a boil, reduce the heat, and simmer for 1 hour. Once the carrots are cooked through, taste to adjust for seasoning and discard the chile.

Transfer the soup to a high-speed blender or use an immersion blender to blend the soup until smooth, making sure the lid is tightly closed when blending. Add the orange and the lemon juice to the blender, again blending until smooth. Serve warm with the desired garnishes. Leftover soup may be stored in an airtight glass container in the refrigerator for up to 5 days.

PURPLE SWEET POTATO SOUP WITH SALTED MUSHROOMS

SERVES 6 ▪ Loaded potato soup served up with shredded cheese, chives, and bacon is very much a representation of my fused German, Scandinavian, British, and Irish family ancestry. I wanted to make this a new family tradition, with a Japanese spin utilizing purple potatoes, that I could enjoy tummyache-free. Blending antioxidant-rich purple sweet potatoes with coconut milk makes this soup creamy, rich, and tasty without adding tons of extra fat, sugar, or heavy cream. The roasted salty mushrooms are a perfect replacement for bacon—drizzled with some olive oil, this combination makes for one satisfying soup.

4 cups chopped button mushrooms

¼ cup balsamic vinegar

4 tablespoons olive oil

Sea salt

1 pound purple sweet potatoes* (about 4 medium)

½ sweet onion, chopped

½ teaspoon ground cinnamon

½ teaspoon ground cumin

¼ teaspoon chili powder

Freshly ground black pepper

2 cups light coconut milk

2 cups filtered water

¼ cup fresh thyme leaves, reserve 1 tablespoon total for garnishing all servings

Juice of 1 lemon

1 tablespoon pure maple syrup

Garnish: olive oil

*Seek out purple sweet potatoes at your local natural foods store or Asian market, or use regular sweet potatoes.

Preheat the oven to 400°F. Line two baking sheets with foil.

In a large bowl, combine the mushrooms, vinegar, 2 tablespoons of the oil, and 1 tablespoon salt and stir to combine. Spread the mixture evenly on one of the lined baking sheets. Arrange the sweet potatoes on the second baking sheet. Place the mushrooms on the bottom rack and the sweet potatoes on the rack above. Bake the mushrooms for 30 minutes, until firm and dry, not crisp. Bake the sweet potatoes for 45 minutes, or until the natural sugars start to caramelize and they are soft when poked with a knife in the center.

In a medium skillet, warm the remaining 2 tablespoons oil over medium heat. Add the onion, 1 teaspoon salt, the cinnamon, cumin, chili powder, and pepper to taste and sauté for 5 minutes, or until the onion is fragrant and translucent.

Transfer the onion and baked sweet potatoes to a high-speed blender and add the coconut milk, water, the ¼ cup thyme, the lemon juice, maple syrup, and salt and pepper to taste. Blend until the soup is thick and creamy. Be sure to have the blender lid on securely before blending. (Alternatively, add the remaining ingredients to a soup pot and blend with an immersion blender.) If you find that it's too thick (not all potatoes will have the same starch content), thin the soup with water. Adjust seasonings to taste.

Serve the soup in bowls, topped with 2 to 3 tablespoons of the mushrooms, a sprinkling of thyme, and a drizzle of olive oil. Serve hot/warm. Store in an airtight glass container in the refrigerator for up to 1 week.

Nutrition Tip: Unlike regular white potatoes, sweet potatoes contain significantly higher amounts of vitamin A, beta-carotene, potassium, and fiber. Beta-carotene and vitamin A, in general, have been shown to be beneficial to eye and cardiovascular health, to protect against certain types of cancer, and to help fight free-radical damage.

EVENING

SUPPER:
TIME TO UNWIND AND DINE

Supper is a special time to unwind and enjoy a warm meal prepared at home; for many of us, it's the last meal of the day and a great way to put a cap on eating for the day. Supper doesn't have to be a laborious activity. Most evenings in my home, supper takes less than 15 minutes to make and is often a combination of meal components I've made on my batch-cooking day the weekend prior. These are recipes like Peppery Tempeh with Polenta (page 204) and Rawlnut Burritos (page 192). But sometimes I want supper to be an activity that I purposefully spend a little extra time and love creating and making. Most often, that happens on the weekend—the perfect time for meals like Beetroot Burgers with Maple Mustard (page 185) and Roasted Vegetable Lasagna with Lemon Raw-cotta (page 183). So get comfortable, relax, and sit and enjoy your last meal of the day in style and with purpose.

ZUCCHINI PIZZA CRUST WITH LEMONY PEA PESTO

SERVES 4 ▪ Zucchini is a surprisingly chameleon-like vegetable—I find myself using it frozen in morning smoothies, pureed in desserts, and, now, grated in pizza crust! Zucchini pizza is a great way to sneak in extra servings of vegetables, and it is naturally lower in carbohydrates and higher in fiber compared with traditional crusts. This recipe pays homage to a cauliflower crust, which is one of my most popular recipes from the blog. Both of these recipe components, the crust and pea pesto, can be enjoyed on their own, yet when combined, it's evident they're meant to be enjoyed together.

3 cups finely grated zucchini

1 to 2 teaspoons sea salt

½ cup almond flour (see page 47)

2 tablespoons brown rice flour (see page 47)

2 eggs, beaten

2 cloves garlic, minced

2 tablespoons nutritional yeast

1 teaspoon dried oregano

½ teaspoon red pepper flakes

Freshly ground black pepper

Olive oil, for drizzling

Lemony Pea Pesto (recipe follows)

Garnishes: arugula, grated fresh lemon zest, fresh lemon juice, and freshly ground black pepper

Place the grated zucchini in a strainer, sprinkle the salt on top, and gently toss until the salt is distributed. Allow the zucchini to sit and sweat excess moisture for 45 to 60 minutes.

Transfer the zucchini from the strainer to a nut-milk bag or cheesecloth. Wrapping the cloth around the zucchini entirely, use your hands to squeeze out any excess liquid. Repeat the process until the zucchini no longer releases liquid. Place the zucchini in a large bowl and add the flours, eggs, garlic, nutritional yeast, oregano, red pepper flakes, and black pepper to taste. Stir to combine well.

Position one rack in the middle of the oven and another in the top position. Place a pizza stone (for a crispier crust) or a baking sheet lined with parchment paper on the middle rack. Preheat the oven to 500°F.

Place a large piece of parchment paper on a clean countertop and drizzle it with olive oil. Spread the

(recipe continues)

(recipe continued from page 174)

zucchini dough onto the parchment paper and form the dough into a large 10-inch round or oval, about ½ inch thick.

Transfer the dough from the parchment paper directly to the hot pizza stone or lined baking sheet and bake for 20 minutes. Flip the pizza crust over and bake for an additional 10 minutes, until the crust is firm-crisp. Carefully remove the crust from the oven, spoon on the pesto to the desired thickness, and bake on the top rack for 5 to 7 minutes, until the pesto is warm. Remove from the oven. Top with garnishes, if desired, and serve immediately.

LEMONY PEA PESTO

MAKES ABOUT 1½ CUPS

  1 (10-ounce) bag frozen peas
  2 tablespoons pine nuts, toasted (see page 42)
  2 cloves garlic, minced
  2 tablespoons olive oil
  2 tablespoons filtered water
  2 tablespoons hemp seeds
  1 tablespoon grated fresh lemon zest
    Juice of 1 lemon
    Pinch of sea salt
    Freshly ground black pepper

Quick-thaw the peas by blanching in boiling water for 3 minutes or microwaving until soft. In a food processor or high-speed blender, combine the peas, pine nuts, garlic, oil, water, hemp seeds, lemon zest, lemon juice, salt, and pepper to taste and pulse until the mixture is well combined and thick. Adjust seasonings to taste. Store in an airtight glass container in the refrigerator for up to 1 week.

GARDEN BEETROOT PIZZA WITH SUNFLOWER SEED PÂTÉ

SERVES 4 · Beets are powerful players in the nutrient-density game; they're high in antioxidants and anti-inflammatory compounds and loaded with a phytonutrient called betanin, which supports our body's natural detoxification system. Beyond their nutritional value, beets also add a beautiful color to whatever meal they're a part of.

This stunning pizza crust may be enjoyed on its own, since it's so doughy and delicious, but I like to step it up by adding more veggies and a protein-rich sunflower seed pâté for added flavor and nutrition. Make sure to soak the seeds for 2 hours before you get started. Enjoy this pizza with friends, over laughs, drinks, and slightly pink-stained hands.

BEETROOT CRUST

- 6 medium red beets, peeled and quartered
- 1 egg
- 1 tablespoon coconut oil
- ½ cup almond flour (see page 47)
- 1 cup brown rice flour (see page 47) or gluten-free all-purpose flour
- 2 teaspoons baking powder
- 2 cloves garlic, minced
- 1 teaspoon dried oregano
- ½ teaspoon sea salt
- Pinch of red pepper flakes
- Olive oil, for baking

TOPPINGS AND GARNISH

- 14 tablespoons tomato paste
- 6 to 8 asparagus spears, cut into 1-inch pieces
- ½ cup sliced mushrooms
- 1 tomato, sliced into rounds
- Sunflower Seed Pâté (recipe follows)
- Handful of watercress or arugula
- 2 soft-boiled eggs, halved lengthwise

For the beetroot crust: Preheat the oven to 400°F. Line a baking sheet with parchment paper.

Place the quartered beets on the baking sheet and roast for 40 minutes, or until fork tender. Set aside to cool to room temperature.

Increase the oven temperature to 500°F and place a pizza stone (for a crispier crust) or a baking sheet lined with parchment paper in the oven on the middle rack.

(recipe continues)

(recipe continued from page 177)

Once the beets have cooled to room temperature, place them in a high-speed blender along with the egg and oil. Puree and set aside.

In a large bowl, combine the almond flour, rice flour, baking powder, garlic, oregano, salt, and red pepper flakes. Add the beet mixture to the bowl and stir to combine. Pour the dough onto a lightly floured surface and knead about 5 minutes, or until the flour is incorporated and the dough is smooth. Lightly grease a sheet of parchment paper with olive oil. Transfer the ball of dough to the parchment paper and, using your hands, press and stretch the dough flat.

Lightly brush olive oil on another piece of parchment paper and place it on top of the hand-flattened dough. Use a rolling pin and work from the center of the dough outward to flatten the dough to a 10- to 12-inch round about ¼ inch thick. Peel off the top parchment paper and place the pizza crust with the bottom parchment paper on the hot pizza stone or lined baking sheet. Bake for 5 minutes, or until the crust is firm to the touch.

Spread the tomato paste evenly over the crust, then add the asparagus, mushrooms, and tomato and bake for 5 to 7 minutes, until the vegetables are just fork tender.

To serve, dollop the sunflower seed pâté on top, add additional seasonings of your choice, garnish with the watercress or arugula, and top with the soft-boiled eggs. Enjoy warm. Keep leftovers in an airtight glass container in the refrigerator for up to 4 days.

Tip: Did you stain your hands while working with the beets? Try rubbing the used lemon halves onto the palms of your hands along with some salt to help fight the stain.

(recipe continues)

(recipe continued from previous page)

SUNFLOWER SEED PÂTÉ

MAKES ABOUT 1½ CUPS ▪ *This pâté can be used as a spread on sandwiches and crackers or as a veggie dip.*

 1 cup raw sunflower seeds, soaked for 2 hours
½ red bell pepper, cored and chopped
 1 large carrot, chopped
 2 tablespoons nutritional yeast
 1 clove garlic
    Juice of 1 lemon
    Pinch of sea salt
    Freshly ground black pepper

In a high-speed blender or food processor, combine the sunflower seeds, bell pepper, carrot, nutritional yeast, garlic, lemon juice, salt, and pepper to taste and pulse until combined. You are trying to achieve a soft but chunky texture. Store in an airtight glass container in the refrigerator for up to 1 week.

ROASTED VEGETABLE LASAGNA WITH LEMON RAW-COTTA

SERVES 8 • This is not your traditional lasagna. I like to make the vegetables and the lemon "raw-cotta" a day ahead. The secret ingredient in the marinara—walnuts—makes this dish both hearty and satisfying while providing a healthful boost of omega-3 fatty acids and protein. You can also enjoy these lasagna components in other recipes by storing the leftovers in the fridge or freezer for a later quick meal for you or your family.

LEMON RAW-COTTA

2 cups raw almonds, soaked overnight

1 cup filtered water

Juice of 2 lemons

2 cloves garlic

Pinch of sea salt

Freshly ground black pepper

ROASTED VEGETABLES

1 large eggplant, thinly sliced lengthwise

2 large zucchini, thinly sliced lengthwise

2 large yellow squash, thinly sliced lengthwise

1 tablespoon olive oil, plus more for drizzling

Sea salt and freshly ground black pepper

2 cups mixed mushrooms, such as white button, shiitake, and portobello

½ large sweet onion, sliced

2 cloves garlic, minced

MARINARA

2 tablespoons olive oil

1 small red onion, diced

3 cloves garlic, minced

1 teaspoon sea salt

1 teaspoon dried oregano

1 teaspoon dried parsley

Freshly ground black pepper

½ cup tomato paste

2 cups tomato sauce or 1 (15-ounce) can

4 cups diced fresh tomatoes or 2 (15-ounce) cans

½ tablespoon blackstrap molasses

½ cup chopped raw walnuts

ASSEMBLY

1 pound gluten-free lasagna noodles

3 cups chopped fresh spinach

1 tablespoon grated lemon zest, for garnish

For the lemon raw-cotta: Peel the almonds. This should be very easy after soaking. Squeeze the soft almonds between your fingers to pop off the skins (discard the skins). Place the almonds in a food processor or high-speed blender with the water, lemon juice, garlic, salt, and pepper to taste and pulse to combine. Taste and adjust the salt. Place cheesecloth over a large mesh strainer set on top of a deep bowl and pour the raw-cotta mixture into the strainer, allowing the liquid to drain through the cheesecloth and into the bowl. Let drain at room temperature for up to 8 hours. Store in an airtight glass container in the refrigerator for up to 1 week.

(recipe continues)

(recipe continued from previous page)

For the roasted vegetables: Preheat the oven to 400°F. Spread the sliced eggplant, zucchini, and yellow squash evenly across several large baking sheets (see Tip). Drizzle with some oil and a pinch each of salt and pepper and bake for 40 minutes.

Meanwhile, in a medium skillet, heat the 1 tablespoon oil over medium heat. Add the mushrooms, sweet onion, and garlic and cook about 10 minutes, or until tender. Set aside.

For the marinara: In a medium saucepan, heat the oil over medium-low heat. Add the red onion and cook until translucent. Add the garlic, salt, oregano, parsley, and pepper to taste and cook for 5 minutes, or until fragrant. Add the tomato paste, tomato sauce, diced tomatoes, and molasses and simmer over low heat for up to 1 hour, or until the sauce has thickened, continually stirring and adjusting seasoning. Add the chopped walnuts and cook for an additional 5 minutes.

For the assembly: Preheat the oven to 350°F. Measure out 1 cup of the marinara sauce and set aside. Spread a thin layer of marinara on the bottom of a 9 x 13-inch baking pan, cover with uncooked gluten-free lasagna noodles, a layer of roasted vegetables, including the chopped spinach, and another layer of sauce. Repeat until all the ingredients are used. Cover with foil and bake for 45 minutes, or until the noodles are tender. Remove the foil and bake for an additional 7 minutes.

To serve, reheat the reserved marinara in a small saucepan. Spread a layer of the raw-cotta on top of the lasagna and sprinkle with the lemon zest, followed by the hot marinara (this will warm the raw-cotta without ruining the texture). Enjoy immediately, or freeze the lasagna for up to 2 weeks.

Tip: For optimal results, place the vegetable slices on a raised wire rack above the pans to help drain excess liquid from the squash and eggplant.

BEETROOT BURGERS WITH MAPLE MUSTARD

SERVES 4 • When transitioning to a whole-food lifestyle that's heavy on the plants, it's convenient to reach for highly processed foods that are made with soy or isolated proteins just to have textures reminiscent of beloved "normal" foods, such as burgers. But by skipping the fake, you'll also forgo harmful chemicals, artificial sweeteners, artificial colorings, preservatives, and questionable binders. These burgers contain heaps of minerals, plant-based proteins, fiber, and powerful antioxidants that help to detoxify the liver. Plus, they flat-out taste awesome. When you bite into this burger, you will become a veggie burger believer!

BEETROOT BURGERS

2 large red beets

1 tablespoon coconut oil

Sea salt and freshly ground black pepper

1 cup filtered water

½ cup white or red quinoa

1 tablespoon olive oil

1 medium sweet onion, diced

3 cloves garlic, minced

1 tablespoon Dijon mustard

1 tablespoon smoked paprika

1½ teaspoons ground cumin

½ teaspoon ground coriander

½ teaspoon dried thyme

½ teaspoon red pepper flakes

2 tablespoons raw apple cider vinegar

1 cup rolled oats

4 cups cooked black beans or 2 (15-ounce) cans, drained and rinsed

¼ cup chopped pitted Medjool dates (about 2)

2 eggs, lightly beaten

4 burger buns (I like the Gluten-Free Sesame Seed Buns, page 188)

MAPLE MUSTARD

¼ cup yellow mustard

2 tablespoons pure maple syrup

½ teaspoon pure maple extract (optional)

Dash of ground cinnamon

Preheat the oven to 350°F.

For the beetroot burgers: Using a vegetable grater, shred the beets into a small bowl and toss with the coconut oil and a dash each of salt and pepper. Spread evenly on a baking sheet and bake for 45 minutes, or until tender. Set aside to cool.

In a small saucepan, bring the water to a boil. Add the quinoa, reduce to a simmer, and cook for 25 minutes, or until the quinoa has absorbed all the water. Set aside.

(recipe continues)

(recipe continued from previous page)

In a medium skillet, warm the olive oil over medium heat. Add the onion and cook for 3 to 5 minutes, until the onion is translucent. Add the garlic, mustard, smoked paprika, cumin, coriander, thyme, red pepper flakes, 2 teaspoons salt, and black pepper to taste. Once this mixture has softened, stir in the vinegar, remove from the heat, and set aside.

In a food processor, process the rolled oats to a fine flour. Empty into a small bowl and set aside. Place the beans in the food processor and pulse. Add the dates and pulse until combined. This mixture will be thick and moist. Scrape the bean mixture into a large bowl.

If there is a lot of moisture from the beets, put the shredded beets into a strainer and squeeze with your hands to remove some of the excess water. Add the cooled beets to the beans and mix. Taste the mixture and adjust seasonings to taste. Add the oat flour, quinoa, and eggs and stir to combine.

Rest the batter in the refrigerator for about 40 minutes, or until all the moisture has been absorbed by the oat flour. If the mixture is still wet, add more oat flour. Use your hands to form 6 patties. You may bake or pan-fry these patties. Freeze extra patties for another use.

- **To bake:** Preheat the oven to 350°F. Place the patties on a baking sheet lined with parchment paper and bake for 30 minutes, or until firm and golden brown on the outside.

- **To pan-fry:** Grease a large shallow skillet with coconut oil and warm over medium-high heat. Cook the burgers on each side for about 4 minutes, or until a nice crust forms.

For the maple mustard: In a small bowl, whisk together the mustard, maple syrup, maple extract (if using), and cinnamon.

Serve the burgers on your favorite bun with some maple mustard and your favorite toppings, such as tomatoes, lettuce, pickles, etc.

GLUTEN-FREE SESAME SEED BUNS

MAKES 4 BUNS • A burger is only as good as its toppings, condiments, and buns. These sesame buns are light and fluffy but include minerals you simply won't find in other buns. They're gluten-free, with the base coming from nuts, seeds, coconut flour, and sesame seeds—all of which are loaded with calcium, iron, and protein. The maca, optional here, adds a bit of earthy flavor, like a whole wheat bun. Trust me, any homemade Beetroot Burger (page 185) you take the time to make deserves to be cushioned in a homemade bun too.

1 cup coarsely ground raw cashews

¼ cup almond flour (see page 47)

⅓ cup coconut flour

1 tablespoon maca powder (optional)

2 tablespoons tahini

3 eggs, separated

1 teaspoon raw apple cider vinegar

1 teaspoon sea salt

¼ cup almond milk or sesame seed milk (see page 45)

4 tablespoons coconut oil, melted, plus more for shaping

1 teaspoon baking soda

¼ cup sesame seeds

Tip: You can make and bake buns ahead of time to freeze for later. Tightly wrap each uncooked bun in plastic wrap before freezing. They will keep in the freezer for 1 month. Defrost before baking.

Preheat the oven to 325°F. Line a baking sheet with parchment paper.

In a high-speed blender or food processor, combine the cashews, flours, maca powder (if using), tahini, egg yolks, vinegar, sea salt, almond milk, and the 4 tablespoons oil and blend until smooth. A sticky dough should form.

Using an electric mixer, beat the egg whites until stiff peaks have formed. Stir the baking soda into the egg whites. Add the egg white mixture to the food processor and pulse with the flour mixture until combined.

Spread a little coconut oil on your hands (about a tablespoon) and form 4 equal balls of dough. Take each dough ball and form it to the shape and size of a hamburger bun, 3 to 4 inches in diameter, and place on the lined baking sheet. These won't spread much while baking, so get them as close together as possible. Gently press the sesame seeds into the buns. Bake for 25 minutes, or until golden brown. Set on a rack to cool fully, and then halve each bun horizontally. Serve immediately.

THREE UN-BUNS

EACH VERSION MAKES 1 BUN • If you're in the mood for something a little less carbohydrate rich, swap out the Gluten-Free Sesame Seed Buns (opposite page) for one of these veggie alternatives: large portobello mushroom caps, thick slices of sweet potato, or simple lettuce leaves, such as butter leaf lettuce or crunchy romaine. All delicious options to try out at your next summer BBQ!

SWEET POTATO BUNS

Preheat the oven to 350°F. Line a baking sheet with parchment paper. Use a sharp knife to cut the widest part of a **large sweet potato** diagonally into 2-inch-thick slices. Lay the potato slices flat on the lined baking sheet, drizzle with **olive oil,** and sprinkle **coarse salt** and **pepper** on top. Bake for 30 minutes, or until tender firm. Use one slice as the top bun, another round as the bottom.

PORTOBELLO MUSHROOM BUNS

Enjoy raw or cooked. To cook, preheat the oven to 350°F. Line a baking sheet with parchment paper. Lay 2 **portobello mushroom caps cap side down** on the lined baking sheet, drizzle with **olive oil,** and sprinkle **coarse salt** and **pepper** on top. Bake for 30 minutes, or until tender-firm. Use one cap as the top bun, the other as the bottom.

LETTUCE BUNS

Take a large leaf of **butter leaf lettuce** or **crunchy romaine** and wrap the lettuce leaf around your burger to act as the bun.

AVOCADO CLUB SANDWICH WITH MARINATED PORTOBELLO MUSHROOMS

SERVES 2 ▪ Meat lovers everywhere will love this vegan sandwich. Portobello mushrooms are thinly sliced and marinated in a savory bold dressing for hours so they soak up the rich flavor. The result is eerily similar to sliced roast beef, and incredible! The creamy avocado serves as a play on mayonnaise, binding all the ingredients together and creating a nice balance of texture and flavors. Try adding a layer of my peppery tempeh (page 204) in this sandwich and prepare to have your taste buds blown.

4 portobello mushroom caps

¼ cup balsamic vinegar

2 tablespoons olive oil

2 tablespoons tamari or nama shoyu

1 tablespoon pure maple syrup

2 cloves garlic, minced

1 tablespoon chopped fresh thyme

1 tablespoon finely chopped fresh rosemary

Sea salt

1 avocado

2 slices Artisan Seeded Bread (page 134)

Garnishes: sliced heirloom tomato, sliced radishes, butter leaf lettuce or arugula, Dijon mustard, pea shoots or sprouts, sea salt, freshly ground black pepper

Using a mandoline or a knife, thinly slice (less than ¼ inch) the portobello mushrooms. In a deep baking dish, combine the vinegar, oil, tamari, maple syrup, garlic, thyme, rosemary, and a pinch of salt. Whisk to combine.

Gently arrange the mushroom slices flat in the baking dish to absorb the marinade. Cover and store in the refrigerator for 2 hours, remove, and stir, flipping the mushrooms over to ensure all the liquid is being evenly absorbed, then re-cover and refrigerate for at least 8 hours. The mushrooms may be stored in an airtight glass container in the refrigerator for up to 5 days.

To serve, mash ¼ to ½ avocado on each bread slice, add a pinch of salt, then evenly layer on the marinated mushrooms. Top with desired garnishes.

Nutrition Tip: Portobello mushrooms contain B vitamins, copper, potassium, phosphorus, selenium, and antioxidants galore. They are particularly great for plant-based diets, adding a hearty or meaty component to the meal.

RAWLNUT BURRITOS

SERVES 4 • Eating foods raw is a great way to retain the highest concentration of nutrients, antioxidants, and minerals. This raw dish gets a kiss of heat from the cayenne and jalapeños. Pico de gallo is a condiment everyone should know how to make with their eyes closed—it's completely refreshing and can be added to almost anything from tacos to salads.

RAWLNUT FILLING

- 1 cup raw walnuts
- ½ cup raw almonds
- 2 tablespoons olive oil
- ¼ cup minced red onion
- 2 cloves garlic, minced
- 1 tablespoon tomato paste
- 1 tablespoon ground cumin
- 1 teaspoon cayenne pepper
- 1 teaspoon sea salt
- Freshly ground black pepper
- ⅓ cup chopped fresh cilantro

ASSEMBLY

- 4 large romaine lettuce leaves
- Pico de Gallo (recipe follows)
- Optional fillings: fresh tomato slices, sliced red onion, sliced avocado, chopped cilantro, sliced jalapeños, Cashew Cheese (page 49)

Nutrition Tip: Tomatoes also contain vitamins C and K, B vitamins, copper, potassium, folate, iron, zinc, and other traces of minerals.

For the rawlnut filling: In a food processor, combine the walnuts, almonds, oil, onion, garlic, tomato paste, cumin, cayenne, salt, and black pepper to taste. Pulse to combine, then taste and adjust seasonings. Gently pulse in the cilantro. The rawlnut filling may be stored in an airtight glass container in the refrigerator for up to 1 week. Enjoy leftovers with salads or sandwiches.

For the assembly: Fill each romaine lettuce leaf with about ½ cup rawlnut filling, as much pico de gallo as you like, and other fillings, if desired. Roll up like a burrito and enjoy!

PICO DE GALLO

MAKES ABOUT 1 CUP

- 3 large tomatoes, diced
- 1 medium red onion, diced
- ⅓ cup chopped fresh cilantro
- 2 jalapeño peppers, chopped
- Juice of 1 lemon
- Juice of 1 lime
- 1 teaspoon minced garlic
- 1 teaspoon sea salt
- Freshly ground black pepper

In a small bowl, stir together all the ingredients. Adjust the salt and black pepper as desired. The pico de gallo may be stored in an airtight glass container in the refrigerator for up to 1 week.

BUDDHA'S NOURISH BOWL

SERVES 1 ▪ This is one of the most loved recipes on my blog. Why? It's a delicious no-fuss one-bowl meal that is rooted in celebrating food as food. Its balance of carbohydrates, healthful fats, and protein-rich ingredients will keep your body fueled and your taste buds completely happy. It's a fun play on a traditional ramen bowl minus the broth.

SESAME-GINGER DRESSING

¼ cup rice vinegar

Juice of 1 orange

½-inch piece fresh ginger, peeled and grated

1 teaspoon tamari or nama shoyu

2 tablespoons sesame seeds, toasted (see page 42)

NOURISH BOWL

¼ cup dried seaweed, such as dulse

Filtered water

1 tablespoon cold-pressed sesame oil

2 cups chopped bok choy

1 cup chopped broccolini

½ cup chopped shiitake mushrooms

½ tablespoon sesame oil

½ cup thinly sliced red bell pepper

¼ cup thinly sliced red onion

2 ounces 100% buckwheat soba noodles, cooked according to package instructions

4 large radishes, thinly sliced

¼ cup canned sliced water chestnuts

2 soft-boiled eggs

¼ cup chopped scallions (white and light green parts)

For the sesame-ginger dressing: In a small bowl, whisk together the vinegar, orange juice, ginger, tamari, and sesame seeds. Set aside.

For the nourish bowl: Soak the seaweed in about 1 cup filtered water for at least 10 minutes, or until soft. Drain and discard the water.

In a large skillet, heat the sesame oil over medium heat. Add the bok choy, broccolini, and mushrooms and cook for 10 minutes, or until wilted.

Purely for presentation purposes, in a large shallow bowl, start with the bok choy as the base, then arrange the mushrooms, broccolini, bell pepper, onion, seaweed, noodles, radishes, and water chestnuts in individual sections. Or, if you prefer, combine all the bowl ingredients with no specific assembly arrangement. Top with the soft-boiled eggs and scallions.

Drizzle the dressing on top and adjust seasonings to taste before serving.

Nutrition Tip: Broccolini is one of many vegetables in the cruciferous family, containing high amounts of vitamin K, vitamin A, chromium, fiber, B vitamins (folate in particular), manganese, calcium, iron, zinc, and selenium.

CARROT GNOCCHI WITH CARROT GREENS PESTO

SERVES 8 · I could easily call this recipe "No Part of the Carrot Left Behind." Often when people purchase carrots, they opt for ones that have already been washed and peeled, missing out on the best part—the greens! Carrot greens are loaded with flavor and nutrients, and they make for the perfect accompanying sauce for this dish. This recipe is a feast for the eyes too: These gnocchi are a rich orangey color, which is a beautiful contrast with the pesto made from the greens.

CARROT GNOCCHI

1 pound carrots with tops, carrot greens removed and reserved for the pesto

1 egg, beaten

1 clove garlic, minced

1 tablespoon olive oil

½ teaspoon sea salt

¼ teaspoon freshly grated nutmeg

¼ teaspoon freshly ground black pepper

2 cups gluten-free flour

2 tablespoons cornstarch

CARROT GREENS PESTO

2 cups carrot greens, well washed

1 cup chopped fresh basil

½ cup pine nuts, lightly toasted (see page 42)

3 tablespoons nutritional yeast

1 tablespoon hemp seeds

Juice of 1 lemon

½ teaspoon sea salt

Freshly ground black pepper

⅓ cup olive oil

For the carrot gnocchi: In a steaming basket, cook the carrots for 10 minutes, or until fork tender. Set aside to cool, then transfer to a food processor and add the egg, garlic, oil, salt, nutmeg, and pepper. Pulse to combine, until the carrots reach a mashed consistency. Set aside in a large bowl.

In a small bowl, combine the flour and cornstarch. Add about two-thirds of this flour mixture to the carrot mash bowl and incorporate just until a dough forms. If this dough is too wet or sticky, add additional flour gradually—be sure not to overwork the dough.

With the remaining flour, dust a clean surface and turn the dough out onto it. Knead the dough, taking care not to overmix. Divide the dough into 4 equal parts, rolling out each into a log about 1 inch wide and ½ inch thick, then cut off ½-inch pieces using a sharp knife. Use a gnocchi board or simply roll the dough pieces on the back of a long three-pronged fork, gently creating the signature gnocchi lines and shape. Be gentle with this process. Repeat until all the remaining dough is finished. You should have 50 or more gnocchi.

(recipe continues)

(recipe continued from page 196)

In a medium pot, bring 6 cups of water to a boil over high heat. Working in batches, place about 10 gnocchi at a time into the pot, being careful not to overcrowd the water or let it boil over. When the gnocchi float to the top, they're finished. Use a slotted spoon to remove and let rest in a bowl. Repeat the process until all the gnocchi are cooked.

For the pesto: In a food processor or high-speed blender, combine the carrot greens, basil, pine nuts, nutritional yeast, hemp seeds, lemon juice, salt, and pepper to taste and blend on low speed. With the machine running, gradually add the oil to the pesto to properly combine until it is smooth. If it's too thick, add water, 1 tablespoon at a time. Adjust seasonings to taste.

Serve the gnocchi warm and spoon the carrot greens pesto on top. Store leftovers in an airtight glass container in the refrigerator for up to 4 days, or freeze the gnocchi without the pesto for up to 2 weeks.

CHEESY NOODLES AND SPRING PEAS

SERVES 4 ▪ Who doesn't love cheese and noodles? As a playful ode to my mother who used to put broccoli or peas in our mac and cheese, I purposefully sneak vegetables into this dish to bump up the nutritional value. The peas in this dish are beautiful pearls of green, bursting with a subtly sweet flavor. Nutritional yeast is the star ingredient here, making these noodles cheesy sans dairy, and as a bonus, it's incredibly rich in B vitamins and protein too.

2 cups cubed butternut squash

8 ounces brown rice elbow pasta

2 cups fresh or frozen green peas, thawed if frozen

1 cup light coconut milk

¼ cup cashews, soaked for 2 hours and drained

1 cup nutritional yeast

2 tablespoons Dijon mustard

1 clove garlic, minced

Pinch of cayenne pepper

Pinch of sea salt

Freshly ground black pepper

In a steaming basket, cook the squash cubes for 20 minutes, or until soft. Transfer to a food processor and puree until smooth. Leave in the food processor and set aside.

In a medium pot, bring 3 cups of water to a boil over high heat. Add the pasta and cook according to the package directions. Add the peas to the boiling pasta water and quick-cook the peas for about 3 minutes. Strain the pasta and peas and then return to the pot.

To the pureed butternut squash, add the coconut milk, cashews, nutritional yeast, mustard, garlic, cayenne, salt, and black pepper to taste. Blend until smooth.

Pour the sauce mixture into the pasta and pea pot and gently stir over low heat to combine. Adjust seasonings to taste. Serve warm and garnish with additional black pepper, as desired.

COCONUT CURRY EGGS

SERVES 4 • Curry is one of my favorite dishes; it's full of flavor and completely satisfying. This one-dish curry saves you heaps of time and ensures that cleanup will be a breeze. It also makes for a beautiful rustic display! Protein-rich eggs and the healthful fats from both the egg yolk and coconut milk are a great combination for satisfying your hunger.

2 tablespoons olive oil

½ cup chopped red onion

3 cloves garlic, minced

2 large zucchini, diced

2 large carrots, chopped

½-inch piece fresh ginger, peeled and minced

½ teaspoon ground coriander

½ teaspoon ground cumin

½ teaspoon ground turmeric

½ teaspoon sea salt

¼ teaspoon cayenne pepper

Freshly ground black pepper

1 cup light coconut milk

1 (15-ounce) can diced tomatoes

4 eggs

Garnishes: chopped fresh cilantro, parsley, or mint; chopped cashews; freshly squeezed lemon juice

Preheat the oven to 350°F.

In a cast-iron skillet, warm the oil over medium heat. Add the onion, garlic, zucchini, carrots, ginger, coriander, cumin, turmeric, salt, cayenne, and black pepper to taste. Stir and cook for 10 minutes, or until tender. Add the coconut milk and tomatoes and bring to a simmer.

One at a time, crack each egg carefully and place in separate parts of the skillet, directly on top of the veg mixture. Transfer the skillet to the oven and bake for 10 minutes, or until the eggs have reached your desired doneness.

Serve over raw salad greens, cooked greens, or warm grains (see page 39). Top with garnishes as desired.

PEPPERY TEMPEH WITH POLENTA

SERVES 2 • Sweet heat is a perfect way to describe the flavor profile of this dish. The sweet comes from the slow-cooked onions and maple syrup, but then the heat from the black pepper, red pepper flakes, garlic, and ginger comes through to warm the back of your throat! Made from fermented soybeans, tempeh is a great option for plant-centric lifestyles, as it's high in protein and contains healthful fats, fiber, and beneficial bacteria, which promote good digestion. The creamy polenta made with coconut milk balances this dish out nicely.

POLENTA

2 cups filtered water

½ teaspoon sea salt

½ cup organic yellow cornmeal

½ cup light coconut milk

Freshly ground black pepper

1 large tomato, diced

¼ cup diced red onion

1 red bell pepper, thinly sliced

1 yellow bell pepper, thinly sliced

⅓ cup chopped fresh cilantro

Juice of 1 lemon

Juice of 1 lime

2 tablespoons olive oil

PEPPERY TEMPEH

3 tablespoons coconut oil

½ medium red onion, thinly sliced

5 cloves garlic, smashed

1 teaspoon red pepper flakes

1½ tablespoons freshly ground black pepper

1 tablespoon minced peeled fresh ginger

3 tablespoons tamari or nama shoyu

3 tablespoons filtered water

2 tablespoons maple syrup or honey

8 ounces tempeh, thinly sliced

For the polenta: In a small saucepan, bring the water to a boil, then add the salt. While whisking gently, pour the cornmeal into the boiling water in a steady stream. Reduce the heat to low and continue whisking for about 10 minutes, until the polenta has thickened enough that it doesn't settle back on the bottom of the pan when you stop stirring and also pulls from the sides of the pan.

Cover the polenta and continue cooking, stirring occasionally, for 35 minutes, making sure to scrape the sides, bottom, and corners of the pan. Stir in the coconut milk as the polenta finishes cooking; it should be al dente in texture and taste. Season with pepper to taste and more salt, if needed. Set aside to cool, then stir in the tomato, onion, bell peppers, cilantro, lemon juice, lime juice, and olive oil.

For the tempeh: In a deep skillet, warm the coconut oil over low heat. Add the onion, garlic, red pepper flakes, black pepper, and ginger. Cook for about 15 minutes, or until the onion and garlic are soft and translucent.

In a small bowl, whisk together the tamari, water, and maple syrup. Set aside.

Add the tempeh to the deep skillet with the cooked onion and spoon the tamari-maple mixture over to coat. Cook for 10 minutes.

To serve, spoon the polenta into a serving dish and top with the tempeh. Serve hot. Store leftovers in the refrigerator in an airtight glass container for up to 4 days.

SIDES:
SMALL PLATES AND THE SUPPORTING CAST

S ides truly bring together a meal; they create balance of flavor and texture, and can bring lightness or heartiness to an entrée. You can easily enjoy them as an entrée as well by adding proteins, healthful fats, or carbohydrates. Most side dishes are either vegetable- or starch-based. I love mixing the two to create a balance. Some of these are classics, but now with a Nutrition Stripped style. My favorites from this bunch include the Acorn Squash Rounds with Dill-Cashew Cream (page 208) and the Southern-Style Skillet Corn Bread (page 218).

ACORN SQUASH ROUNDS WITH DILL-CASHEW CREAM

SERVES 4 TO 6 • Delicata squash is hands-down my favorite of all the winter squashes. I know that's a bold statement, but after trying this recipe using delicata or acorn (more available) squash for yourself, you'll totally get it. Rich in fiber and vitamin A, acorn and delicata squash have a texture similar to that of butternut squash, and an edible skin similar to a zucchini's, making it the perfect vehicle for delivering the dill-cashew cream.

DILL-CASHEW CREAM

1 cup raw cashews, soaked for 2 hours and drained

½ cup filtered water

¼ cup chopped fresh dill

¼ cup chopped sweet onion

2 cloves garlic

Juice of 1 lemon

1 teaspoon sea salt

Freshly ground black pepper

SQUASH ROUNDS

2 acorn squash

2 tablespoons olive oil

Pinch of sea salt

Pinch of ground cumin

Pinch of cayenne pepper

Freshly ground black pepper

Tip: Try the dill-cashew cream as a replacement for mayonnaise on sandwiches, or as a dip for other vegetables.

For the dill-cashew cream: In a high-speed blender, combine the cashews, water, dill, onion, garlic, lemon juice, salt, and pepper to taste and blend until smooth. Adjust the salt and black pepper to taste. Pour the cream into a small serving dish for dipping and set aside. Place in the refrigerator if you want a chilled dip.

For the squash rounds: Preheat the oven to 400°F. Line 2 baking sheets with parchment paper.

Slice the squash crosswise into ½-inch-thick rounds (it's easier to slice the squash before it's been seeded). Using a spoon, gently scoop out the seeds from the centers of the squash slices. Place the squash rounds on the baking sheets, drizzle with the oil, and sprinkle with the salt, cumin, cayenne, and black pepper to taste. Bake for 30 minutes, or until golden and firm. Flip the squash rounds over at the 15-minute mark.

Serve the squash warm with the dill-cashew cream alongside for dipping. Leftover squash rounds may be stored in an airtight glass container in the refrigerator for up to 5 days, but store the cream in a separate airtight glass container. Reheat squash upon serving again.

SWEET POTATO WEDGES WITH CURRY KETCHUP

SERVES 4 · In this recipe, I boost the vitamin A and antioxidants in my favorite side dish, fries, by baking sweet potatoes instead of regular ole white potatoes. I then pair them with an Indian twist on an American classic condiment, ketchup. If you've never made ketchup before, now's the time to start! Allowing the ingredients to simmer for an hour results in a rich, creamy sauce with bold tomato flavors. Stir in the curry spice blend and you've got some of the best ketchup you'll ever try.

4 large sweet potatoes (about 4 inches in diameter)

2 tablespoons coconut oil, melted

1 tablespoon ground cinnamon

1 teaspoon sea salt

Freshly ground black pepper

Curry Ketchup, for serving (recipe follows)

Preheat the oven to 350°F.

Line a baking sheet with parchment paper.

Halve the sweet potatoes lengthwise, then cut each half into 4 pieces so you have 8 wedges per potato. Place the wedges in a large bowl and toss with the oil, cinnamon, salt, and pepper to taste. Spread the potato wedges on the baking sheet so that none overlap—this will ensure that each one browns. Bake for 45 minutes, flipping the potato wedges halfway through for even baking, until fork tender and firm on the outside.

Serve the potatoes warm with the ketchup on the side at room temperature or slightly warmed. Store in an airtight glass container in the refrigerator for up to 1 week.

(recipe continues)

(recipe continued from previous page)

CURRY KETCHUP

MAKES ABOUT 1 CUP

2 cups whole peeled tomatoes or 1 (15-ounce) can
½ cup pure maple syrup
½ cup filtered water
¼ cup chopped sweet onion
2 tablespoons tomato paste
1 teaspoon mustard
2 cloves garlic, minced
1 teaspoon sea salt
½ teaspoon freshly ground black pepper
2 tablespoons Curry Spice Blend (recipe follows)

In a medium saucepan, combine the tomatoes, maple syrup, water, onion, tomato paste, mustard, garlic, salt, and pepper and bring to a boil over medium heat. Boil for 10 minutes, then reduce the heat to a simmer and cook for 1 hour, or until the ketchup easily coats the back of a wooden spoon. Continue simmering for 30 to 45 minutes, allowing the ketchup to further reduce in volume.

Pour into a high-speed blender (or use an immersion blender) and blend until smooth. You may choose to strain out any of the additional tomato pulp at this point. Let the ketchup cool, then adjust the salt and pepper to taste. Add the curry spice blend to the ketchup mixture. Stir to combine, taste, and add more spice, if desired. Ketchup may be stored in an airtight glass container in the refrigerator for up to 1 week.

CURRY SPICE BLEND

MAKES ABOUT ½ CUP

2 tablespoons ground cumin
2 tablespoons ground cardamom
¼ cup ground turmeric
1 tablespoon mustard powder
1½ teaspoons cayenne pepper

In a small bowl, stir together all the spices. Store in a small mason jar.

CARROT YOGURT WITH CURRY GRANOLA

SERVES 2 TO 4 • I have a hunch this recipe might be one of the stars of the book! The carrot yogurt alone is enough to hype up, but when coupled with the granola it's ridiculously good, like weak-in-the-knees good.

4 large carrots, chopped

1 tablespoon olive oil

1 tablespoon pure maple syrup

1 cup full-fat coconut milk, chilled overnight

1 cup coconut meat (from 1 fresh young coconut; see Note, page 105)

¾ cup fresh coconut water or almond milk (see page 45)

4 probiotic capsules (see page 288), opened

Juice of 2 lemons

2 teaspoons honey

Pinch of sea salt

¼ cup Curry Granola (recipe follows), for serving

Preheat the oven to 400°F. Line a baking sheet with parchment paper.

In a large bowl, toss the carrots with the oil and maple syrup. Spread the carrots evenly onto the prepared baking sheet and roast for 35 minutes, until soft and sweet. Let cool completely.

Transfer the cooled carrots to a high-speed blender. Add the chilled coconut milk, coconut meat, coconut water, probiotics, lemon juice, honey, and salt and blend until smooth. Divide the mixture among 2 to 4 glass jars, depending on how many servings you wish to make, and set at room temperature. Allow the yogurt to naturally ferment for 24 hours, then chill the fermented yogurt in the refrigerator before serving. The yogurt will keep in the refrigerator for up to 1 week.

Serve ¼ cup of granola over each serving of yogurt.

(recipe continues)

(recipe continued from previous page)

CURRY GRANOLA

MAKES ABOUT 5 CUPS

1½ cups rolled oats

1 cup raw almonds

1 cup raw sunflower seeds

1 cup raw pumpkin seeds

½ cup raw chopped walnuts

⅓ cup flaxseeds

2 tablespoons Curry Spice Blend (page 212)

1 teaspoon ground cardamom

1 teaspoon ground cinnamon

1 teaspoon ground turmeric

½ teaspoon cayenne pepper

Pinch of sea salt

2 ripe bananas

3 tablespoons pure maple syrup

1 tablespoon coconut oil

2 tablespoons tahini

Preheat the oven to 350°F. Line a baking sheet with parchment paper.

In a large bowl, combine the oats, almonds, sunflower seeds, pumpkin seeds, walnuts, flaxseeds, curry spice blend, cardamom, cinnamon, turmeric, cayenne, and salt.

In a food processor or high-speed blender, combine the bananas, maple syrup, coconut oil, and tahini and mix until smooth. Pour this wet mixture into the granola bowl and stir until well coated.

Spread the granola evenly on the lined pan and bake for 15 minutes. Break up the granola mixture into smaller clusters and bake another 10 to 15 minutes, until golden brown. Let cool completely, about 1 hour, before storing in an airtight glass container at room temperature. This will keep for several weeks.

BLACK RICE RISOTTO WITH MUSHROOMS

SERVES 4 TO 6 • Black rice coupled with mushrooms creates an incredibly earthy, natural, and organic vibe for this comforting risotto. I enjoy making this dish most on the weekends, when I have time to give a little extra attention and love to it—the constant stirring is meditative and quite therapeutic!

4 cups vegetable stock

2 tablespoons olive oil, plus more for drizzling

1 cup black rice

1 small sweet onion, diced

2 cups diced portobello mushrooms

2 cups diced white button mushrooms

2 cups diced shiitake mushroom caps

2 tablespoons minced fresh thyme

1 tablespoon minced fresh sage

1 tablespoon minced fresh rosemary

2 cups dry red wine

Garnishes: fresh rosemary sprigs, olive oil, sea salt, freshly ground black pepper

In a saucepan, bring the stock to a boil, then keep at a simmer. In a large pot, heat 1 tablespoon of the oil over medium heat. Add the rice, toasting until fragrant, no more than 2 minutes. Add 1 cup of the hot stock to the rice. Cook, stirring constantly, until all the liquid has been absorbed. Continue adding 1 cup of stock at a time, until all the liquid has been absorbed and the rice is tender—this can take up to 1 hour.

In the meantime, in a large skillet, warm the remaining 1 tablespoon oil over medium heat. Add the onion, mushrooms, and herbs. Sauté for 10 minutes, or until the mushrooms have begun to cook and release some of their juices, then add the red wine to deglaze the pan. Add the mushroom mixture to the risotto and stir until combined.

Serve the risotto warm with fresh rosemary sprigs on top, a drizzle of oil, and a pinch of salt and pepper.

Nutrition Tip: Black rice contains high levels of anthocyanin antioxidants, even more than blueberries! It also contains copper, iron, and other trace minerals as well as fiber and protein.

SOUTHERN-STYLE SKILLET CORN BREAD

SERVES 12 • Corn bread just isn't corn bread without pops of sweet corn kernels encased in a crumbly cake with a delicate balance of sweet and savory flavors. My Southern-style corn bread has a hint of sweet, but recipe variations will allow you to make it as savory or spicy as you like. Whichever way you choose, this side is a hit and goes well with Chocolate-Cinnamon-Walnut Chili (page 161), Baked Sticky Fig BBQ Beans (page 222), or any other dish that was made to be soaked up!

2 cups plus 2 tablespoons cornmeal

1 cup brown rice flour (see page 47)

2 teaspoons baking powder

1 teaspoon sea salt

¼ teaspoon freshly grated nutmeg

Freshly ground black pepper

2 cups light coconut milk

2 tablespoons pure maple syrup

⅓ cup grapeseed oil

1 tablespoon raw apple cider vinegar

Optional add-ins (see variations)

1 cup frozen corn kernels, thawed

Preheat the oven to 350°F. Grease a 9- or 10-inch cast-iron skillet or 13 × 9-inch baking pan.

In a large bowl, mix together 2 cups of the cornmeal, the flour, baking powder, salt, nutmeg, and pepper to taste. In a medium bowl, whisk together the coconut milk, maple syrup, oil, and vinegar. Stir in one of the optional add-ins if using.

In a small bowl, toss the corn kernels with the remaining 2 tablespoons cornmeal to coat, then add to the dry ingredients. Add the wet mixture to the dry ingredients and stir until well combined.

Pour the batter into the prepared skillet and bake for 30 to 35 minutes, until a toothpick inserted into the center comes out clean. Cut into slices, squares, or simply break apart a serving with your hands.

To change up the flavor of your corn bread, add one of the following to the wet ingredients when making the batter:

·½ cup chopped fresh chives + ½ cup chopped jalapeños
·⅓ cup chopped fresh rosemary, thyme, and sage
·⅓ cup chopped apricots + ⅓ cup chopped fresh rosemary
·⅓ cup chopped fresh cilantro + ¼ cup salsa

TURMERIC AND GARLIC ROOT MASH

SERVES 4 • Move over mashed potatoes—this mash utilizes celeriac (a.k.a. celery root) and turnips, delicious yet often overlooked root vegetables. Celeriac may look like something out of a Tim Burton movie, but it is tasty and as versatile as a potato. Turmeric gives this root mash a beautiful golden color and bold flavor when mixed with roasted garlic. Enjoy this mash on a plate mixed with roasted vegetables or as a bed for peppery tempeh (page 204) or some other type of hearty protein.

2 medium yellow potatoes, chopped

5 turnips, peeled and chopped

1 celeriac, peeled and chopped

2 teaspoons ground turmeric

1 teaspoon sea salt

Freshly ground black pepper

3 tablespoons olive oil

1 head garlic

½ cup light coconut milk

Preheat the oven to 400°F. Line 2 baking sheets with parchment paper and set aside.

In a large bowl, combine the potatoes, turnips, celeriac, turmeric, salt, and pepper to taste. Drizzle on the oil and toss with your hands to coat. Spread the vegetable mixture out evenly onto the baking sheets. Slice the garlic head about ¼ inch from the bottom to expose the individual cloves. Add the bulb to one of the baking sheets, then place both sheets in the oven and bake for 40 minutes, or until soft.

Allow the garlic bulb to cool slightly, then gently squeeze until the cloves come out of their skins; squeeze into a food processor or high-speed blender. Transfer the roasted vegetables to the processor or blender and blend until just smooth. Add the coconut milk and blend until velvety smooth or pulse to leave it as chunky as desired.

BAKED STICKY FIG BBQ BEANS

SERVES 6 • In the South, baked beans are a *thing*. And in my home state, Ohio, baked beans are always the dish to bring to family picnics, summer barbecues, and even winter gatherings. To avoid refined sugars, I sweeten the beans with fiber-loaded figs, which also thickens it, and the molasses provides a boost of iron. I have a hunch you'll enjoy this barbecue sauce, not just with beans but with tofu, tempeh, fish, and whatever else you might crave.

2 tablespoons coconut oil

2 cloves garlic, minced

½ medium red onion, diced

1 shallot, diced

3 large tomatoes, chopped (about 3 cups)

1 cup dried figs or 2 cups chopped fresh figs

1 teaspoon freshly ground black pepper

1 teaspoon ground cumin

1 teaspoon sea salt

Pinch of red pepper flakes, or to taste

½ cup filtered water

4 tablespoons tomato paste

1 tablespoon Dijon mustard

2 heaping tablespoons blackstrap molasses

¼ cup raw apple cider vinegar

2 cups vegetable stock, plus 1 cup more if needed

Cayenne pepper (optional)

1 cup cooked butter beans or ½ (15-ounce) can, drained and rinsed

1 cup cooked cannellini beans or ½ (15-ounce) can, drained and rinsed

1 cup cooked kidney beans or ½ (15-ounce) can, drained and rinsed

In a large saucepan, warm the oil over medium heat. Add the garlic, onion, and shallot and cook for 5 minutes, until translucent. Add the tomatoes, figs, black pepper, cumin, salt, red pepper flakes, and water. Bring the mixture to a boil and cook for about 15 minutes.

Add the tomato paste, mustard, molasses, vinegar, and stock and use an immersion blender (or transfer to a stand blender) to blend until smooth. Return the mixture to the saucepan and simmer over low heat for 2 hours, stirring occasionally. Adjust the seasoning for spice and heat. I like adding extra heat with cayenne or more red pepper flakes. The end result will be a thick and sticky sauce; if it's too thick, you may add an extra cup of stock. The sauce may be stored in an airtight glass container in the refrigerator for up to 2 weeks.

Preheat the oven to 350°F.

In a 13 × 9-inch baking dish, combine the beans and sauce, stirring until well coated. Bake for 20 minutes, or until warmed through and thickened. Serve warm or hot as a side dish. Leftovers may be stored in an airtight glass container in the refrigerator for up to 1 week.

CORN ON THE COB WITH TAMARIND-DATE CHUTNEY

SERVES 4 · My family often serves corn on the cob with butter, salt, and maybe a fleck of fresh chives or parsley. I wanted to bring an international flavor to an American staple, and this chutney spread does just the trick. Tamarind paste is a sweet and tangy spice widely used in Indian cooking. Here, I combine it with dates for a sweet and sticky chutney that has an incredible punch of flavor. When mixed with salt and fresh herbs and smothered over juicy savory corn, it's just magnificent.

4 ears fresh corn, unshucked

2 tablespoons olive oil

Dash of cayenne pepper

Pinch of sea salt

Freshly ground black pepper

Tamarind-Date Chutney (see page 125)

Preheat the oven to 350°F.

Place the corn, still in the husks, directly on any oven rack and roast for 25 minutes, or until the corn is soft. Using an oven mitt, peel down the husks, then drizzle the corn with oil and sprinkle on the cayenne, salt, and black pepper to taste. Tie the husks in a knot to use as a handle when eating, then put the corn back in the oven for 5 minutes.

To serve, use a brush or a spoon to slather the chutney on the corn.

Note: When consuming corn, corn products, and ingredients that contain corn, search for brands with non-GMO and organic varieties of corn.

MOROCCAN MARINATED ZUCCHINI NOODLES

SERVES 4 • Zucchini noodles are one of the most unique ways to prepare a vegetable. You'll use a special tool called a spiralizer or a good ole vegetable peeler. Zucchini noodles are flexible and have an al dente texture when eaten raw. In this dish, they're marinated in an energizing citrus dressing with fresh herbs and seasonings—it is refreshingly sublime in the warmer months of the year. Adjust the heat to your liking by spiking or reducing the amount of red chile.

4 large zucchini

2 satsumas or clementines, peeled

¼ cup olive oil

Juice of 1 lemon

2-inch piece fresh ginger, peeled

2 cloves garlic

Fresh red chile (1 inch long), seeded, if desired

⅓ cup chopped fresh parsley

⅓ cup chopped fresh cilantro

12 to 15 shredded fresh mint leaves to taste

1 teaspoon ras el hanout

Pinch of sea salt

Freshly ground white pepper

Garnishes: handful of green pea sprouts, crushed pistachios and cashews, chopped fresh mint, chickpeas

Create zucchini noodles with a spiralizer according to your model's instructions or peel the zucchini lengthwise into noodles using a vegetable peeler. Place the noodles in a large bowl and set aside.

In a high-speed blender, combine the satsumas, oil, lemon juice, ginger, garlic, chile, parsley, cilantro, mint, *ras el hanout*, salt, and white pepper to taste. Blend until combined.

Pour the dressing over the zucchini noodles, stir to combine, and adjust the seasonings to taste. Let sit at room temperature for 1 hour or overnight in the refrigerator to marinate. Serve chilled or at room temperature with desired garnishes. Leftovers may be stored in an airtight glass container in the refrigerator for up to 3 days.

Note: Use zucchini noodles in place of cold pasta or other noodles to make a refreshing raw dish, and one that also contains much more fiber than the pasta version. You can also gently warm the noodles and serve with, say, marinara sauce.

RAW SWEET ONION FLAX KNÄCKEBRÖD

SERVES 12 ▪ Get ready to become addicted to the most delicious, crunchy, sweet, salty, savory crackers ever. *Knäckebröd* is a traditional Swedish crisp bread. I've made it completely raw and grain-free by dehydrating a combination of pureed onions, flaxseeds, and sunflower seeds with pungent flavorings that only amplify when dried. The result is a crispy flax cracker that can be enjoyed with crudités of fresh fruit and vegetables, smothered with The Only Hummus You'll Ever Need (page 137) or sweet Chia Jam (page 48), as an accompaniment to a salad or meal, crushed like croutons on top of soup or salad, or savored with a simple hard-boiled egg for a snack.

2 tablespoons pure maple syrup

½ cup olive oil

3 ounces tamari or nama shoyu

3 pounds sweet red onions (about 5 medium), chopped

1 cup ground flaxseeds

1 cup ground sunflower seeds

2 teaspoons ground cumin

Freshly ground black pepper

In a small bowl, whisk together the maple syrup, oil, and tamari. Set aside.

In a food processor, puree half of the chopped onions and transfer to a large bowl. Add the remaining chopped onions, the flaxseeds, sunflower seeds, cumin, and pepper to taste. Add the oil mixture and stir to combine. The texture will be wet and pulled together.

Using an oven: Preheat the oven to 200°F or your lowest oven setting. Grease 4 rimmed baking sheets with coconut oil. Spread the mixture evenly onto the baking sheets and bake for 8 to 10 hours, stopping halfway to flip the dough and cut it into 3-inch squares (for ease of separating later), until the crackers are crisp.

Using a dehydrator: Spread the entire mixture evenly onto four separate dehydrator sheets lined with a

(recipe continues)

(recipe continued from previous page)

silicone pad and dehydrate on 115°F for 8 hours, or until crisp, checking periodically for doneness. About 4 hours in, use a sharp knife to draw lines into the dough; this will make it easier to break into squares after the crackers have completely dehydrated. (Alternatively, you can dehydrate overnight. Skip the cracker-cutting step and flip the bread over first thing in the morning, then continue dehydrating until the cracker is crisp.)

Crackers may be stored in an airtight glass container at room temperature for up to 2 weeks.

Nutrition Tip: Onions contain B vitamins, manganese, vitamin C, copper, and other trace minerals. Like other sulfur-rich foods such as garlic, they have been shown to help the body detoxify and repair free-radical damage. They are also beneficial in promoting cardiovascular health.

APRICOT CARROT CASSEROLE (PORKKANALAATIKKO)

SERVES 8 TO 10 • *Porkkanalaatikko,* Finnish for "carrot bake," is the name of a delicious casserole traditionally served during the holidays. I often gravitate toward making my own Nutrition Stripped spin on traditional British, Irish, German, and Scandinavian dishes. In the substitution of all substitutions, I replace heavy cream, butter, and milk with pureed fresh apricots! The apricots contribute a creaminess that gives this casserole a pudding-like texture. When they are mixed with carrots, coconut milk, and rice, then topped with crunchy maple-crusted nuts and shredded coconut, your taste buds will consider themselves blessed.

8 medium carrots, chopped into 1-inch pieces

½ cup filtered water

1 cup Arborio rice

2 cups light coconut milk

6 large fresh apricots

1-inch piece fresh ginger, peeled

2 eggs

Juice of 1 lemon

2 tablespoons blackstrap molasses

1 tablespoon coconut oil

1 teaspoon ground cinnamon

½ teaspoon ground cardamom

½ teaspoon ground turmeric

Pinch of freshly grated nutmeg

1½ teaspoons sea salt

¼ teaspoon ground black pepper

½ cup chopped raw pistachios

½ cup chopped raw hazelnuts

½ cup rolled oats

¼ cup unsweetened shredded coconut

1 tablespoon olive oil

1 tablespoon pure maple syrup

Preheat the oven to 400°F. Grease a baking sheet with coconut oil.

Arrange the carrots evenly on the baking sheet and roast for 20 minutes, or until fork tender. Let the carrots cool for 15 minutes. (Leave the oven on.)

Meanwhile, in a medium saucepan, bring the water to a boil. Add the rice and cook, stirring until the water has been completely absorbed. Add the coconut milk ½ cup at a time and bring the mixture to a boil after each addition, stirring constantly so the porridge doesn't burn at the bottom, until the liquid has been absorbed. Repeat this process until all the coconut milk is gone, 20 to 30 minutes, then set the porridge aside.

(recipe continues)

(recipe continued from previous page)

Transfer the cooled carrots to a high-speed blender and add the apricots, ginger, eggs, lemon juice, molasses, coconut oil, cinnamon, cardamom, turmeric, nutmeg, salt, and pepper and puree. Pour the carrot puree into the saucepan with the rice porridge and stir until combined well.

Grease a casserole pan with coconut oil. Transfer the carrot porridge mixture to the pan. Bake for 1 hour, or until the batter is set and cooked.

Meanwhile, in a large bowl, combine the pistachios, hazelnuts, oats, and shredded coconut and stir to combine.

Take the carrot casserole out of the oven and evenly crumble the oat-nut mixture on top. Drizzle the olive oil and maple syrup on top. Return to the oven and bake for 5 minutes, or until toasted. Serve warm.

DESSERTS:
THE GRAND FINALE

Desserts shouldn't be off limits or thought of as "guilty" pleasures or carry any negative connotation at all. They are simply dishes that put your sweet tooth to rest and allow you to indulge in balance. All my dessert recipes are made entirely of whole foods and sweetened only by natural ingredients like fruit, dried fruit, maple syrup, or honey, so you can feel good about treating yourself. Be sure to try my personal favorites, Raw Sundae with Cocoa-Date Syrup (page 236) and Classic Vanilla Cake with Chocolate Ganache (page 245) and the crowd-pleaser Vanilla Matcha Cream Raw-eos (page 239). Many of the ingredients I use are not only naturally sweet, but they also contain a balance of fiber, protein, and healthful fats, all of which help keep your blood sugars stable so you'll feel just as good after eating as you did before. Sit back, relax, grab a spoon or fork, and enjoy!

RAW SUNDAE
WITH COCOA-DATE SYRUP

SERVES 2 ▪ Growing up, I had to stand guard over my ice cream sundae or risk my brother eating it all up when I wasn't looking. So I've been serious about my dessert for a long time. I can confidently say this sundae is one of a kind, as it contains frozen zucchini! Before you start turning the page, hear me out: The frozen zucchini has a neutral flavor but adds fiber, bulk, and texture to this dessert. With the addition of frozen banana and coconut milk, this is one delicious thick and creamy ice cream sundae. The cocoa-date syrup is so sweet and chocolaty that someone in your life is bound to want to run off with bites of this recipe.

COCOA-DATE SYRUP

- 4 Medjool dates, pitted (7 for a supersweet version)
- 2 tablespoons almond butter (see page 43)
- 2 tablespoons pure maple syrup
- 2 tablespoons coconut oil, melted
- 2 tablespoons cocoa powder

BANANA ICE CREAM

- 2 frozen bananas
- 2 cups chopped frozen zucchini
- ½ cup light coconut milk
- 1 teaspoon pure vanilla extract
- Pinch of sea salt
- Garnishes: toasted coconut, pinch of ground cinnamon, fresh berries, dried mulberries, cherries, cacao nibs, chopped walnuts or almonds

For the cocoa-date syrup: In a high-speed blender, combine the dates, almond butter, maple syrup, oil, and cocoa powder and blend until smooth. Scrape into a medium bowl and set aside. Rinse the blender with warm water to quickly clean. (Store leftover syrup in an airtight glass container in the refrigerator for up to 1 week.)

For the ice cream: In the same blender, combine the bananas, zucchini, coconut milk, vanilla, and salt and blend until smooth, scraping down the sides while blending. (Ice cream should only be made at the time of serving; do not store in the freezer.)

Scoop the ice cream into bowls and drizzle with the date syrup. Garnish as desired and serve immediately.

VANILLA MATCHA CREAM RAW-EOS

MAKES 15 COOKIES • All the raw ingredients in this recipe form a delicious nut- and seed-rich chewy sandwich cookie that cushions a vanilla matcha cream filling; for extra decadence, there's an optional chocolate coating. This is the perfect recipe to showcase matcha tea in a dessert application; it's mixed with cashews and dates and creates a stunning green filling. But you can also leave out the matcha for a more classic cookie (see variation).

VANILLA MATCHA CREAM

2 teaspoons matcha tea powder

¼ cup boiling filtered water

¼ cup coconut oil, melted

3 tablespoons pure maple syrup

1 cup raw cashews, soaked for 2 hours and drained

2 Medjool dates, pitted

2 teaspoons pure vanilla extract

Pinch of sea salt

RAW-EO COOKIES

½ cup chopped pitted Medjool dates (4 to 5)

¾ cup almond flour (see page 47)

1 tablespoon almond butter (see page 43)

⅓ cup ground flaxseeds

½ cup rolled oats

1 tablespoon coconut oil

¼ cup cocoa powder

Pinch of sea salt

2 tablespoons cacao nibs (optional)

CHOCOLATE COATING (OPTIONAL)

1 cup cocoa powder

½ cup coconut oil, melted

2 tablespoons pure maple syrup

½ teaspoon pure vanilla extract

Pinch of sea salt

For the matcha cream: In a small heatproof bowl, combine the matcha and boiling water. Once the tea cools, transfer it to a high-speed blender and add the oil, maple syrup, cashews, dates, vanilla, and salt and blend until smooth. Chill in the refrigerator until it thickens enough to coat the back of a spoon and is spreadable.

For the cookies: Soak the dates in boiling water for 3 minutes to soften, then drain and transfer to a high-speed blender. Add the almond flour, almond butter, flaxseeds, oats, oil, cocoa powder, and salt. Blend until combined. If using cacao nibs, stir in by hand. The mixture should be clumpy but will stick together when pressed with your fingers.

(recipe continues)

(recipe continued from previous page)

Scrape the entire mixture out onto a large sheet of parchment paper. Top with another sheet of parchment paper and roll the dough out so it is ½ inch thick. Remove the top sheet of parchment and use a 2-inch round cutter to cut out the cookies. Re-roll the scraps and cut out more cookies until all the dough is used. You should wind up with about 30 cookie halves (for 15 sandwich cookies in total).

To assemble the cookies, spoon about 1 tablespoon of the filling on one cookie half and gently press another cookie half on top, wiping excess filling from the sides. Repeat until all the cookies have been filled.

For the optional chocolate coating: You can enjoy the cookies now or take them to the next level by adding a chocolate coating. In a medium bowl, combine the cocoa powder, oil, maple syrup, vanilla, and salt and mix well. The consistency should be thick enough to coat the back of a spoon.

Spread out a sheet of parchment paper and place a wire rack over it. Place the cookies on the rack and gently spoon about 1 tablespoon of the chocolate coating on top of each one. The parchment paper will catch any drips. Refrigerate to harden and enjoy chilled.

Classic Vanilla Raw-eos: Omit the matcha and boiling water from the vanilla matcha cream recipe.

———

Nutrition Tip: Matcha tea is high in antioxidants, amino acids, and chlorophyll, the latter of which is responsible for its beautiful bright green color. Of the amino acids contained in matcha tea, L-theanine is the most prominent and is known to have a relaxing effect on the mind and body (possibly because it increases serotonin, dopamine, GABA, and glycine levels in the brain) while the subtle caffeine content creates focus. This might explain why traditionally monks would sip matcha tea to help prepare their minds for meditation.

GERMAN CHOCOLATE CAKE SQUARES

SERVES 12+ • As I'm writing this, my grandpa has just celebrated his ninety-fifth birthday. Amazing, yes! He attributes his longevity and health to taking daily walks and eating prunes each morning. Duly noted, Grandpa. I wonder if it also has something to do with enjoying German chocolate cake for his birthday every year. Needless to say, this recipe was wholeheartedly inspired by my grandpa, his love of chocolate, coconut, pecans, and living a life that's in balance. My recipe mimics traditional German chocolate cake in that it's very rich, dense, and a little goes a long way!

CHOCOLATE CAKE

1 cup brown rice flour (see page 47)

½ cup almond flour (see page 47)

1 cup cocoa powder

2 tablespoons arrowroot powder

2 teaspoons baking soda

1 teaspoon baking powder

1 teaspoon sea salt

½ cup coconut oil, melted

1 cup coconut sugar

1 cup unsweetened applesauce

1 cup freshly brewed coffee

½ cup pure maple syrup

3 eggs, at room temperature, lightly beaten

1 teaspoon pure vanilla extract

1 cup almond milk (see page 45)

1 tablespoon raw apple cider vinegar

COCONUT-PECAN FILLING

½ cup pitted Medjool dates (4 to 5)

2 cups unsweetened shredded coconut

1 cup chopped raw pecans

1 (13.5-ounce) can full-fat coconut milk

3 tablespoons coconut oil

1 tablespoon pure maple syrup

1 teaspoon pure vanilla extract

Garnish: ½ cup unsweetened coconut flakes, toasted

For the chocolate cake: Preheat the oven to 350°F. Line a 12 × 16-inch rimmed baking sheet or sheet pan with parchment paper, grease with oil, then dust with flour.

In a large bowl, combine the flours, cocoa powder, arrowroot powder, baking soda, baking powder, and salt. In a small bowl, combine the oil, coconut sugar, applesauce, coffee, maple syrup, eggs, and vanilla. In a separate small bowl, mix together the almond milk and vinegar.

(recipe continues)

(recipe continued from previous page)

Pour the wet ingredients into the dry ingredients and stir to combine. Gently fold in the almond milk–vinegar mixture with a rubber spatula. Pour the batter onto the prepared sheet pan and evenly spread. Bake for 30 to 35 minutes, until a toothpick inserted into the center comes out clean. Transfer to a wire rack to cool completely, at least 1 hour, before assembling.

For the coconut-pecan filling: In a high-speed blender, combine the dates, coconut, pecans, coconut milk, coconut oil, maple syrup, and vanilla and blend until smooth.

To assemble, transfer the cake from the sheet pan to a serving platter. Using a fork, gently poke holes all over the cake, creating pockets for the filling to fall into. Pour and evenly spread the coconut-pecan filling on top, then sprinkle the toasted shredded coconut on top.

To serve, cut the cake into squares. Serve at room temperature or chilled. Leftovers may be stored in an airtight glass container in the refrigerator for up to 1 week.

CLASSIC VANILLA CAKE WITH CHOCOLATE GANACHE

MAKES 1 DOUBLE-LAYER CAKE ▪ There's a patient waiting game with baking cake—waiting for it to bake, then to cool before icing, then inevitably waiting for the right time to eat it! Spongy classic vanilla cake layered with a lush chocolate filling and topped with chocolate ganache will seriously have you question whether this is dairy-free. Pictured is a cake made from doubling the recipe. You could also top with Coconut Whipped Cream (page 248), fresh berries, and toasted coconut.

CLASSIC VANILLA CAKE

- ¾ cup brown rice flour (see page 47)
- ¼ cup almond flour (see page 47)
- 2 tablespoons arrowroot powder
- 2 teaspoons baking powder
- ¼ teaspoon sea salt
- ¾ cup coconut sugar
- ¼ cup coconut oil, melted
- 3 eggs
- 1 teaspoon pure vanilla extract
- ½ cup almond milk (see page 45)

CHOCOLATE GANACHE

- 8 ounces unsweetened chocolate, chopped
- ¾ cup full-fat coconut milk
- 1 tablespoon coconut oil
- 1 tablespoon pure vanilla extract
- 1 cup pure maple syrup
- Pinch of sea salt
- 1 teaspoon instant espresso powder

CHOCOLATE FILLING

- 2 cups raw cashews, soaked for 2 hours and drained
- ¼ cup filtered water

Preheat the oven to 350°F. Line the bottoms of two 9-inch round cake pans with rounds of parchment paper. Grease the paper with coconut oil and dust with brown rice flour.

For the cake: In a medium bowl, whisk together the flours, arrowroot powder, baking powder, and salt. Set aside.

In a large bowl, using an electric hand mixer on medium speed, beat the coconut sugar and oil for 5 minutes, or until light and fluffy. Add the eggs one at a time, beating well after each addition. Add the vanilla and almond milk and mix on medium until combined. Gently pour the flour mixture into the bowl with the wet ingredients and beat until well combined.

(recipe continues)

(recipe continued from previous page)

Evenly divide the batter between the two cake pans; they will be thin layers. Bake for 25 minutes, or until a toothpick inserted into the center comes out clean. Let the cakes cool for at least 30 minutes in the pans on a rack. Turn the cakes out of the pans onto the rack to cool completely, about 2 hours.

For the ganache: In a double boiler top over simmering water, combine the chocolate, coconut milk, oil, vanilla, maple syrup, salt, and instant espresso. Stir constantly until fully melted and smooth. (Ganache may be stored in an airtight glass container in the refrigerator for up to 1 week. If made ahead, rewarm to pouring consistency for coating this cake. Try it as a topping for other desserts or coconut milk yogurt, or use it as a dip for fruit.)

For the filling: In a high-speed blender, combine ½ cup of the ganache with the soaked cashews and water and blend until light and fluffy. Pour into a small bowl and refrigerate until you're ready to assemble the cake.

To assemble the cake, place one of the cooled cake layers on the wire rack, spread the chocolate filling evenly over the top, then carefully place the second layer on top. Completely frost the cake with the filling, then pour the remaining chocolate ganache over the cake and let cool before serving.

RAW PEACH TART WITH COCONUT WHIPPED CREAM

SERVES 12 • One of the most recognized recipes from my blog, this tart is beautiful, simple to make, and delicious. Plus you can swap peaches with any other fruit that's in season: Try pears, thinly sliced apples, apricots, strawberries—the possibilities are endless!

Raw Tart Shell (recipe follows)

3 cups peach slices (about 4 peaches)

Juice of 1 lemon

Honey, for drizzling

Coconut Whipped Cream (recipe follows)

Make the tart shell and freeze as directed.

Arrange the peach slices in the tart shell in a circular pattern, similar to a rose. Sprinkle the top with the lemon juice and then drizzle on some honey.

Serve wedges of the tart with a dollop of the coconut whipped cream. Store the tart in the refrigerator for up to 1 week, covered with plastic wrap or foil.

RAW TART SHELL

MAKES ONE 10- OR 12-INCH TART SHELL

1 cup raw almonds

1 cup raw walnuts

½ cup raw pecans

½ cup raw cashews

6 Medjool dates, pitted

1 tablespoon grated fresh lemon zest

1 teaspoon ground cinnamon

½ teaspoon sea salt

1 tablespoon coconut oil

In a nut grinder or food processor, grind the nuts until finely textured; leaving a couple small chunks is fine. In a food processor or high-speed blender, place all the ground nuts along with the dates, lemon zest, cinnamon, salt, and coconut oil and blend on

(recipe continues)

(recipe continued from previous page)

medium speed until a sticky dough forms. It should hold together when pressed between your fingers—if your mixture is too wet or moist, add more ground nuts.

Using a 10- or 12-inch tart pan with a removable bottom (or a springform pan), press the raw dough into the pan and up the sides. Press firmly until a shell is formed. Chill the tart shell in the freezer for at least 2 hours or refrigerate overnight.

COCONUT WHIPPED CREAM

MAKES ABOUT 1 CUP

- 1 can full-fat coconut milk, chilled overnight
- 1 tablespoon pure maple syrup
- ½ teaspoon pure vanilla extract
- Pinch of sea salt
- 1 tablespoon grated fresh lemon zest (optional)

Flip over the coconut milk can to the opposite end from the one it was stored on. This will leave the thick coconut cream at the bottom of the can and the liquid coconut milk at the top so you can pour off the liquid part. Open the can, pour off the liquid, and reserve for another use (like a smoothie; see pages 79 to 93). You're now left with the thick cream; this is what you will be using to create the whipped cream.

Transfer the coconut cream to a glass jar with a lid. Add the maple syrup, vanilla, salt, and lemon zest (if using). Close the jar tightly and shake vigorously for 3 to 5 minutes to "whip" the cream. Store the coconut whipped cream in the jar in the refrigerator for up to 4 days.

PUFFED RICE CARAMEL COOKIES

MAKES 20 COOKIES • These healthful yet wonderful cookies remind me of so many treats: classic Rice Krispies Treats, Star Crunches, and caramel corn, just to name a few. But instead of being junk food, my crispy treats are fiber and protein rich from the dates, sunflower seeds, pecans, and almond butter. This cookie is unlike most cookies—it's chunky, sticky and best eaten chilled, and it requires no baking whatsoever. Cookies for the non-baker!

1 cup coarsely chopped raw sunflower seeds, lightly toasted (see page 42)

½ cup finely chopped raw pecans, lightly toasted (see page 42)

2 cups coarsely chopped puffed brown rice

Dash of ground cinnamon

1 teaspoon sea salt

1 cup pitted Medjool dates (about 9)

⅓ cup almond butter (see page 43)

2 tablespoons coconut oil

1 teaspoon pure vanilla extract

Line a baking sheet with parchment paper, grease with coconut oil, and set aside. In a large bowl, combine the sunflower seeds, pecans, puffed rice, cinnamon, and salt.

In a small bowl, soak the dates in boiling water to cover for 3 minutes to soften. Reserving the soaking water, drain the dates. Transfer the dates to a food processor and puree, adding some of the soaking water to thin.

Transfer the date puree to a medium saucepan. Add the almond butter, oil, and vanilla and warm over medium heat until bubbles start to form. Remove from the heat and immediately pour over the dry ingredients.

Using oil-greased hands, mix the cookie dough until combined. Take about 2 tablespoons of the mixture into your hands and roll into a ball. Place the ball on the parchment-lined baking sheet and flatten with the palm of your hand. Repeat with the remaining mixture.

Place the baking sheet of cookies in the refrigerator to cool for 1 hour, or until firm (these cookies do not require any baking, just time to set). Enjoy chilled or at room temperature. Store in an airtight glass container in the refrigerator for up to 1 week or in the freezer for up to 1 month.

SALTED CARAMEL BROWNIES

MAKES 12 BROWNIES • "These are actually good for you?" That is the most common question I get from friends who've eaten my many recipes, but it's most often asked about these brownies in particular. Made with 100 percent whole food ingredients, these brownies are ooey-gooey, sweet, and salty. Flaxseeds magically transform into an egg replacement and simultaneously increase the omega-3 fatty acids and fiber, while keeping the brownies incredibly moist and decadent. The caramel sauce is divine—and you can easily use it for other recipes and desserts.

1 cup gluten-free all-purpose flour

1 cup almond flour (see page 47)

½ cup cocoa powder

2 tablespoons arrowroot powder

½ teaspoon baking powder

½ teaspoon baking soda

½ teaspoon sea salt

2 tablespoons ground flaxseeds

6 tablespoons filtered water

¾ cup coconut sugar

⅔ cup semisweet chocolate chips

½ cup pure maple syrup

⅓ cup coconut oil, melted

¼ cup full-fat coconut milk

1 teaspoon instant espresso dissolved in 1 tablespoon boiling water

2 teaspoons pure vanilla extract

Caramel Sauce (recipe follows)

Coarse sea salt, for garnish

Preheat the oven to 350°F. Line a 9 × 9-inch baking pan with parchment paper.

In a large bowl, combine the flours, cocoa powder, arrowroot powder, baking powder, baking soda, and salt. Place the ground flaxseeds in a small bowl and stir in the water. Soak for at least 10 minutes, or until a gel has formed.

In a small saucepan, combine the coconut sugar, chocolate chips, maple syrup, oil, coconut milk, dissolved instant espresso, and vanilla. Warm over medium heat to melt the chocolate, stirring until smooth, and remove from the heat.

In a food processor or high-speed blender, blend together the melted chocolate mixture with the flaxseed gel. Gradually add this wet mixture to the dry ingredients and stir until combined.

Pour the batter into the lined baking pan and bake for 30 to 40 minutes, until firm or a toothpick inserted into the center comes out clean.

While the brownies are in the oven, make the caramel sauce. Just as the brownies come out of the oven, use a knife to score the top about ¼ inch deep, and pour the caramel on top, allowing it to settle into the cracks. Sprinkle the top with coarse sea salt to taste. Enjoy warm or set on a wire rack to cool to room temperature before serving.

_____

CARAMEL SAUCE

MAKES ABOUT 1 CUP ▪ *You can also enjoy this sauce with fresh fruit or ice cream (page 236).*

- ½ cup pure maple syrup
- ½ cup coconut oil
- ⅓ cup plus 2 tablespoons almond butter (see page 43)
- 1 teaspoon vanilla extract
- 2 Medjool dates, pitted
- 1 tablespoon honey
- ¼ teaspoon sea salt

In a high-speed blender, combine the maple syrup, oil, almond butter, vanilla, dates, honey, and salt and blend until thick and smooth. Store in an airtight glass container in the refrigerator for up to 1 week.

_____

LEMON COOKIE AND STRAWBERRY-RHUBARB ICE CREAM SANDWICHES

MAKES 6 SANDWICHES • Ice cream sandwiches, universally loved, are one of my favorite summer treats. Rhubarb, on the other hand, is a vegetable that doesn't get enough credit. It's a good source of potassium, and when it's mixed with its classic counterpart, strawberries, which are high in vitamin C, a unique tart and sweet flavor results. This combo is best known in pie but is equally delicious in this soft-serve ice cream. Sandwiched in between chewy lemon cookies, this is one serious summer treat!

STRAWBERRY-RHUBARB ICE CREAM

- 3 cups chopped rhubarb
- 3 tablespoons coconut sugar
- 2 tablespoons filtered water
- 1 large ripe banana
- 2 cups strawberries, fresh or thawed frozen
- 2 tablespoons coconut oil, melted
- 3 tablespoons pure maple syrup
- Juice of 1 lemon
- 1 teaspoon pure vanilla extract
- Pinch of sea salt

LEMON COOKIES

- 2 cups almond flour (see page 47)
- ½ cup unsweetened shredded coconut
- 1 teaspoon baking powder
- ½ teaspoon baking soda
- ½ teaspoon sea salt
- 2 tablespoons grated fresh lemon zest
- 2 tablespoons freshly squeezed lemon juice
- ½ cup honey
- 2 eggs
- 1 teaspoon pure lemon extract
- 1 tablespoon pure vanilla extract

For the ice cream: In a medium saucepan, combine the rhubarb, coconut sugar, and water and cook over medium heat for 20 minutes, stirring occasionally, until the rhubarb is soft. Transfer the mixture to a high-speed blender and blend until smooth, then pour into a bowl to chill in the refrigerator for 2 hours.

Scrape the chilled rhubarb puree into a high-speed blender. Add the banana, strawberries, oil, maple syrup, lemon juice, vanilla, and salt and blend until smooth and creamy. Pour into a freezer-safe container and chill overnight in the freezer or, if you can't wait, for 2 hours.

(recipe continues)

(recipe continued from previous page)

For the lemon cookies: Preheat the oven to 350°F. Line 2 baking sheets with parchment paper.

In a large bowl, combine the almond flour, coconut, baking powder, baking soda, and salt. In a separate bowl, whisk together the lemon zest, lemon juice, honey, eggs, lemon extract, and vanilla until smooth. Add the wet mixture to the dry ingredients and stir until well combined.

Using a tablespoon, drop the batter evenly onto the prepared baking sheets; repeat with all the batter to make 6 cookies on each baking sheet. Bake for about 15 minutes, or until a toothpick inserted into a cookie comes out clean. Transfer to a rack to cool completely. Place the cookies on a baking sheet or tray and chill in the freezer for no more than 20 minutes.

To assemble the ice cream sandwiches, place 2 to 3 tablespoons of the ice cream between two pieces of parchment paper and flatten using the palm of your hand. Place the flattened ice cream disk between two of the chilled cookies. Serve immediately or wrap tightly in plastic wrap and store in the freezer for up to 1 week.

CHOCOLATE FUDGE PALETAS

MAKES 6 PALETAS · Paletas are a kind of ice pop and are essential summer treats no matter what time of day. All you need is a high-speed blender and an ice pop mold. This recipe is similar to a Fudgsicle but contains none of the heavy cream and refined sugars. The star ingredient is avocado—and the result is a beautiful thing!

1 cup light coconut milk

½ cup cocoa powder

3 tablespoons pure maple syrup

1 tablespoon instant espresso powder

2 avocados

Pinch of sea salt

In a small saucepan, heat the coconut milk, cocoa powder, maple syrup, and instant espresso over medium heat, stirring to combine. Pour this mixture into a high-speed blender, add the avocado flesh and the salt, and blend until smooth. Adjust the salt and maple syrup to taste.

Pour the mixture into ice pop molds, leaving about a ¼-inch space at the top. Place the mold covering on top, and gently slide a wooden ice pop stick into each opening. Freeze overnight. To serve, run the molds under hot water just enough to loosen the paletas and enjoy.

PRACTICES AND PLANS TO NOURISH LIFE-LONG HABITS

Whether you're exploring the whole foods lifestyle for the first time or need a fresh start to reboot your habits, these practices and plans make it easy to create habits that seamlessly integrate into your lifestyle.

RULES TO COOK BY

I'll be the first to say, I'm not a chef, nor have I ever claimed to be . . . but I do love teaching myself how to cook by learning skills from the pros, chefs who inspire me, and a simple process of trial and error! I've made plenty of mistakes in recipe development, but these are the moments in which you learn the most. You learn what flavors mesh well together, how to layer seasonings, what textures and knife techniques work with each fruit or vegetable, and how to trust your intuition in the kitchen and let loose. Here are some of the things I've learned along the way:

1. HAVE FUN AND DON'T TAKE YOURSELF TOO SERIOUSLY. I often hear clients and readers getting caught up in the details of measurements, stressing out about cooking techniques, and ultimately disconnecting themselves from the food at hand. There's plenty of fun to be had during cooking, and the more fun you have with it the more often you'll do it!

2. MEASURE ONLY WHEN NECESSARY. While baking requires a fair amount of precision, cooking can be an art and I urge you to consider recipes as guidelines and let your taste buds guide you the rest of the way. If you're a beginner in the kitchen or trying a recipe for the first time, I do recommend following recipes more closely, if not to the letter, until you've gained some confidence.

3. TRUST YOUR KITCHEN INTUITION. This is one of my biggest rules. Allow your mind-body awareness to trickle into the kitchen; use this intuition to cook

from the heart and naturally flow from one task to another.

4. CONSIDER COOKING AS THERAPY. For me, cooking can be completely meditative and relaxing after a really long day of work or whatever else is going on in life. Turn on some tunes, dance around, and let loose.

5. BE CREATIVE. Let your inner artist and creativity loose while cooking, styling, tasting, and adding ingredients to please what your taste buds are craving.

6. AIM FOR BALANCE. As much as I preach about balance in your lifestyle, it also pertains to the kitchen. Each dish should aim to have a balance of components, a balance in flavor (acid, sweet, savory, umami, bitter, earthy, etc.), and a balance in textures (creamy, crunchy, spongy, crispy, starchy, light, etc.).

7. LISTEN TO YOUR BODY. Cook meals and recipes that are nourishing to your body and inner self in that moment. Listen in—it'll tell you!

8. BE RESOURCEFUL. Making a meal and missing an ingredient? Take a look in your pantry, refrigerator, and freezer and try to find a suitable replacement.

9. KNOW YOUR STAPLES! Have several go-to meals during the week that are easy to prepare, you know you'll enjoy eating, and are completely satisfying. See the "My Staples" box for the meals whose ingredients I always keep on hand.

MY STAPLES

Buddha's Nourish Bowl (page 195)

Coconut Milk Yogurt (page 105)

The Only Hummus You'll Ever Need (page 137)

Citrus Creamy Ginger Green Smoothie (page 80)

Turmeric Milk (page 69)

---

10. PERFECT THESE THREE RECIPES. For instant "hostess with the mostess" status, learn how to make these dishes with ease for the next time you have an impromptu guest. No one has to know you didn't spend all day cooking: Artisan Seeded Bread (page 134), Cashew Cheese (page 49), Moroccan Tomato-Chickpea Stew with Walnut Gremolata (page 162).

11. COOK SEASONALLY. Opt for fresh ingredients from your region. Chances are they'll be more affordable and better tasting, and they'll support local farmers.

12. **LEARN THE BASICS.** Learning "The Basics" (page 31) will make your life much easier and your time in the kitchen more enjoyable.

13. **HAVE A GOOD APRON, BECAUSE YOU MIGHT GET MESSY.** Don't say I didn't warn you—when making anything with beets or turmeric (Beetroot Pink Smoothie Bowl, page 88; Beetroot Burgers, page 185; or Turmeric Milk, page 69), chances are you'll make a beautiful mess!

14. **ALWAYS LAYER.** Layer seasonings, taste as you go, and adjust seasonings again. My recipes often instruct, "Adjust to taste." That's because I want you to taste the food as you go along—that's the only way you'll harness your kitchen intuition and learn what goes with what and how to improve dishes with ease.

15. **THE NOSE KNOWS AND SO DO YOUR TASTE BUDS.** Your senses, especially your nose and taste buds, are crucial to helping you determine what seasonings and adjustments to make to your dish. Also, when you're picking fruit and vegetables, these are great senses to call upon.

16. **STOCK YOUR KITCHEN WITH THE RIGHT EQUIPMENT.** Having reliable equipment can take any dish from good to sublime—it's all in the details, whether making precision cuts with knives, pureeing a smoothie until velvety using a high-speed blender, or pulsing nuts or seeds for a flour using a food processor. All a worthwhile investment in your health!

**TOP 10 TOOLS
EVERY NUTRITION
STRIPPED WHOLESOME
KITCHEN NEEDS**

Chef's knife

Cast-iron skillet

Vitamix or other high-speed blender

Food processor

Nut-milk bag/cheesecloth

Dutch oven

Measuring cups and spoons

Spatula

Baking sheet

Mandoline

---

17. **SET YOUR INTENTION.** Who you're cooking for can dramatically change the presentation of a dish, the love that goes into it, and the time/effort put in; it goes with the intention of love. Setting a positive and loving intention while you're cooking is key to nourishing yourself and those you're cooking for on multiple levels.

18. PRESENTATION MATTERS . . . SOMETIMES. Granted, I take a lot of pictures of my food for Instagram, but in reality, my meals sometimes look like a random mix. Presentation matters when you're entertaining, when you want to make a meal feel extra special for yourself or a loved one . . . or on the off chance you're also photographing your food!

19. MULTITASK LIKE A PRO. Most dishes require multiple steps, so if you can learn how to multitask like a boss, you'll be more efficient with your time. I can often juggle ten recipes at once (yes, I've had a little practice). Give it a try on your batch-cooking day (see pages 269-73).

20. CLEAN UP AS YOU GO. Managing multiple recipes at a time is far easier when you keep the clutter at bay. Keep a "clear space, clear mind" mentality.

21. KEEP IT SIMPLE. Recipes don't have to be complex or exhausting to be delicious. My favorite recipes are those that take the least amount of time, thought, and effort but focus on the high quality of ingredients. Deliciously simple!

22. ENJOY THE PROCESS!

BATCH COOKING

What is batch cooking? Basically, it's preparing most or all of your meals and snacks for the entire week on one day out of the week. Simply make a date with your kitchen for one to two hours, one day every week, and have some fun cooking! In my world, it's on Saturdays, right after I finish putting away my morning grocery shopping haul. There's no freezing required, as you'll be consuming everything before the week's end by simply reheating and assembling the meals.

With 168 hours in a week, spending 1 to 2 hours a week for cooking is not asking much, especially if living well is a priority! If you find yourself coming home from work every night and cooking on the fly, it could easily add up to 30 to 60 minutes every evening—that's more than 7 hours a week! We all can use that extra 5 hours a week saved by batch cooking on the weekends to enjoy our time with loved ones, play more, take walks, engage in hobbies, and decompress.

At first, you may feel a bit overwhelmed with all the foods you want to make for an entire week, so I suggest starting out with one meal that you find poses the most challenge for cooking. Ask yourself, "What meal is really difficult for me to cook?" or "What time of day am I most in a time crunch to eat something healthful?" Most of my clients start with supper or breakfast. Start with that meal you've identified to be a challenge and gradually build upon the days'/weeks' worth when you're feeling more comfortable, or jump right in full force! The more often you engage in batch-cooking meal prep, the better and more efficient you'll become at it. Before long, you'll be a master meal-prep machine.

Still not convinced batch cooking is for you? Here are four reasons to start today:

1. Saves you time

2. Keeps you on track with your health and wellness goals

3. Eliminates the mental burden of "What am I going to make for supper (sigh)?" or "I still have to cook (grunt)"

4. Diversifies your food and meal choices throughout the day and week

Batch cooking is a bit of a therapeutic time for me. It's when I can get into what my family and friends call "the zone." I turn on some tunes and cook, blend, and bake as much as my little heart desires. You'll find your groove and have fun with it! Cook these foods naked (i.e., no dressing, no oil, no sauces, limited seasonings, etc.). Then, when mealtime rolls around, simply reheat and add on "toppers"—the sauces, dressings, and dips you've made as well as seasonings and herbs. This is where all the fun and variety happens.

BATCH COOKING, FOR ONE (OR MORE)

Most of my recipes are designed to serve two to six, but I get that many of you may be cooking for just one or two; in my case, this is

---

BATCH-COOKING SUPPLIES

Glass containers or BPA-free plastic containers

Sandwich- and snack-size reusable BPA-free plastic bags

Glass jars with airtight lids

Multiples of certain pieces of equipment, such as baking sheets, pans, and so on

Counter space or extra side tables

BATCH-COOKING STAPLES

Stripped Green Smoothie (page 82)

Coconut Milk Yogurt (page 105)

Homemade nut/seed milks (see page 45)

Buckwheat Stacks (page 107)

Large tossed salad (hold the dressing for now)

Salad dressing (see page 37)

Carbohydrates and starches: cooked brown rice, wild rice, quinoa, millet, sweet potatoes, plantains

Animal proteins: chicken salad, egg salad, tuna salad, chicken breasts/strips (baked, grilled, broiled)

Vegetarian proteins: lentils, chickpeas, black beans, navy beans, black-eyed peas, organic tempeh, organic tofu

Soups (page 157)

Nut or seed butters (page 43)

Lacinato Kale Chips (page 127)

Ultimate Energy Seed Truffles (page 118)

Sliced vegetables and fruits

all the time! So here's how I personally manage batch cooking for most weeks. If you're planning on making a recipe that serves four but you need to cook for only yourself, then know that this recipe will create four meals for you; similarly, a breakfast recipe serving two will feed one for two mornings. So you can make seven servings of the Buckwheat Bircher Muesli (page 111) to feed you for the entire week (use different variations to keep your taste buds happy).

If you're batch cooking for a family, plan out your week of family meals (see Weekly Menu Inspiration, below), using ingredients you have on hand or by making a grocery list to help guide you.

WEEKLY MENU INSPIRATION

These recipes can easily be made in advance, they keep well as leftovers, and they're versatile (i.e., they're easy to vary according to individual preferences).

Breakfast

Buckwheat Bircher Muesli (page 111)

Sweet Potato Julius (page 90)

Mango and Turmeric Lassi (page 91)

Blackberry Sumac Sunflower Seed Muffins with Citrus Cream (page 103)

Sides

Southern-Style Skillet Corn Bread (page 218)

Corn on the Cob with Tamarind-Date Chutney (page 225)

Baked Sticky Fig BBQ Beans (page 222)

Moroccan Marinated Zucchini Noodles (page 226)

Main Options for Lunches or Suppers

Cheesy Noodles and Spring Peas (page 200)

Avocado Club Sandwich with Marinated Portobello Mushrooms (page 191)

Chocolate-Cinnamon-Walnut Chili (page 161)

Zucchini Pizza Crust with Lemony Pea Pesto (page 176)

Peppery Tempeh with Polenta (page 204)

Sweets to Share

Raw Peach Tart with Coconut Whipped Cream (page 247)

Salted Caramel Brownies (page 252)

Raw Sundae with Cocoa-Date Syrup (page 236)

MEAL TRAIN MEALS

These are great meals to make for a friend or loved one when they need a little extra help around the house, whether she's just had a baby or has been out of town, or you want to return a favor, or you simply want to share the love of your cooking with someone. All the recipes below make several servings, which are great for sharing with a family or providing leftovers for one! I highly recommend purchasing a set of glass or BPA-free plastic containers to gift so your friends can keep these leftovers for the week or freeze them for later.

Morning

Salads

Hearty Soups

Mains, Sides, and Desserts

MEAL PLANNING

Planning meals isn't just for dietitians; you can use this skill in your kitchen each week to prepare for a busy week, to share meals with others, or to give your body a reboot!

3-DAY REBOOT AND RESET

Whenever I feel like I've slipped up on healthful habits, I just want to reset and reboot from the inside out. This 3-Day Reboot and Reset (see chart on page 276) is nothing dramatic—there are no juice fasting or smoothies-only restrictions involved. Instead, the plan includes all easy-to-digest foods, nutrient-dense recipes, and a couple of my essential lifestyle tips to get you back on track and help you feel amazing again.

I like to schedule these resets during the change of seasons, when everything in nature is going about its way changing too; for me, it brings a connection with something greater and allows time for reflection and introspection. But maybe your body is aching for a rest after a holiday or vacation that was laden with overly heavy foods. Whatever the reason, take the time to be good to yourself and enjoy good and good-for-you food along the way.

PRE- AND POSTWORKOUT NUTRITION

Whether you consider yourself a serious or recreational athlete, or even a newbie to fitness, everyone can improve their level of health by properly fueling their beautiful bodies! If you're like me, I take my workouts pretty seriously—it's a way for me to get my day off to an amazing start, set my intention, destress, and refocus my

3-DAY REBOOT AND RESET

	DAY 1	DAY 2	DAY 3
UPON WAKING	Warm water with freshly squeezed lemon, ginger tea, or green tea. If you enjoy coffee, I recommend sticking to no more than 1 cup of fair-trade, organic coffee. Immunity Tonic *(page 72)* Probiotics *(optional)*	Warm water with freshly squeezed lemon, ginger tea, or green tea. If you enjoy coffee, I recommend sticking to no more than 1 cup of fair-trade, organic coffee. Immunity Tonic *(page 72)* Probiotics *(optional)*	Warm water with freshly squeezed lemon, ginger tea, or green tea. If you enjoy coffee, I recommend sticking to no more than 1 cup of fair-trade, organic coffee. Immunity Tonic *(page 72)* Probiotics *(optional)*
BREAKFAST	Citrus Creamy Ginger Green Smoothie *(page 80)* If still hungry, follow with a bowl of Buckwheat Bircher Muesli *(page 111)* with almond or nut/seed milk *(see page 45)*	Golden Ginger Honey Smoothie *(page 92)* If still hungry, follow with a bowl of Super Seed Cereal *(page 109)* with almond or nut/seed milk *(page 45)*	Beetroot Pink Smoothie Bowl *(page 88)* If still hungry, follow with a bowl of Oatmeal Porridge *(page 115)* with almond or nut/seed milk *(page 45)*
LUNCH	Moroccan Marinated Zucchini Noodles *(page 226)* with hemp seeds or protein of your choice	Massaged Beet, Carrot, and Brussels Sprout Salad with Citrus-Tahini Dressing *(page 146)*	Zinger Warming Soup *(page 168)*
SUPPER	Rawlnut Burritos *(page 192)*	Turmeric Lemon Broth with Corona Beans *(page 158)*	Moroccan Marinated Zucchini Noodles *(page 226)* with your choice of protein
DESSERT, NIGHTTIME	Mushroom Tonic *(page 76)*	Beauty Papaya Potion *(page 75)*	Turmeric Milk *(page 69)*
SNACKS THROUGHOUT THE DAY, BUT ONLY IF YOU'RE HUNGRY	Garden Pineapple *(page 63)* Coconut Milk Yogurt *(page 105)* Fresh fruit or fresh vegetables	Lacinato Kale Chips *(page 127)* Immunity Tonic *(page 72)* Fresh fruit or fresh vegetables	Energy in a Glass *(page 66)* Fresh fruit or fresh vegetables

energy (or, at times, burn off extra energy). After my morning workouts, I can continue the day with 100 percent focus, intention, and energy and end it with a restful night's sleep, not to mention reap all the amazing health and metabolism benefits of working out in the morning—the after burn. So often I have both clients and readers ask me about nutrition for sports and what to eat before and after working out and how to optimize their energy, results, and time spent in the gym. Here are general guidelines to keep in mind before and after your workout.

Preworkout

Carbohydrate focused. Eat this meal 15 to 40 minutes before exercise.

Ideally, consume a preworkout meal (see below) that's easy on digestion (i.e., won't negatively affect your performance) and gives you quick yet lasting energy.

If you work out in the morning, eat this meal upon waking: ½ to 1 piece fruit + ½ to 1 serving protein (this can be a Nutrition Stripped–approved protein shake).

If you work out in the afternoon, you've most likely already had a half-day of meals. Opt for ½ to 1 piece of fruit or any preworkout foods (see below) depending on the duration of your workout.

If you work out in the evening and/or it's been more than 2 hours since your last meal, eat ½ to 1 carbohydrate serving.

Postworkout

Carbohydrate and protein focused. Eat this meal 30 to 60 minutes after exercise.

Ideally, consume a whole-foods meal containing greens + carbohydrates + quality protein (or two quality proteins if you're vegetarian or simply wish to eat plant-based proteins) + a little fat.

Contrary to what the media says, we don't need to chug a protein shake directly after a workout to get the benefits of working out, to rebuild muscle tissue, or to aid in recovery. What matters most is a steady flow of high-quality and nutrient-dense foods throughout the day, with special attention to surrounding your workouts with protein and carbohydrates.

Consume a postworkout meal (see page 278) at least 1 hour after your workout along with plenty of water to rehydrate.

Preworkout Meal Inspiration (adjust to your goals and portions):

Garden Pineapple (page 63)

Watermelon Herb (page 56)

1 banana or 1 cup fresh fruit or 2 to 4 pitted dates or ¼ to ½ cup dried fruit

½ cup oatmeal made with almond milk (see page 45) or filtered water

1 slice Artisan Seeded Bread (page 134) with a sprinkle of ground cinnamon

½ to 1 baked sweet potato

1 cup coconut water

Postworkout Meal Inspiration (adjust to your individual needs):

Replenish Smoothie (page 87) + a protein

Açaí Berry Bowl (page 84) + a protein

Chocolate Coconut Chip Smoothie (page 93) + a protein

Sweet Potato Julius (page 91) + a protein

Buckwheat Bircher Muesli (page 111) or Oatmeal Porridge (page 115) or Buckwheat Stacks (page 107) with 3 tablespoons hemp seeds or served with 2 to 3 eggs

2 slices Artisan Seeded Bread (page 134) with scrambled eggs (2 whole eggs + 2 egg whites or more depending on your protein goals) cooked with 1 teaspoon coconut oil

1 cup coconut water with 1 cup fruit blended with 1 scoop of your favorite plant-based protein powder

SICK DAY

We've all been there before, whether it's catching the flu from a friend, burning yourself out with stress, not taking enough time to balance your lifestyle and relax, or seasonal allergies. We all need a meal plan to use to keep our immune systems strong. The recipes below are full of nutrient-dense foods, high in antioxidants, anti-inflammatory compounds, warming spices, vitamin C, and minerals, and they are easy on the digestion. Couple these meals with lots of water, tea, and rest, and you'll be set.

Morning

Opt for Golden Ginger Honey Smoothie (page 92), or if you're in the mood for something easy on your throat or digestive system, Beetroot Pink Smoothie Bowl (page 88). Both are high in antioxidants. Fresh ginger can soothe nausea and help generate heat from within, and beets help promote digestion.

Go with the citrus-honey Buckwheat Bircher Muesli (page 111) if you're in the mood for something warm. Vitamin C–rich citrus and antimicrobial honey are a winning combination.

Snacks

Try Elderberry Lime Infusion (page 70) or Immunity Tonic (page 72). Elderberries have been shown to reduce inflammation and the duration of colds and flus owing to their high vitamin C content and antioxidants—and they are also incredibly delicious! Immunity Tonic is loaded with antioxidants and turmeric, which help fight inflammation. The honey will coat and soothe your throat.

Have Coconut Milk Yogurt (page 105) with fresh raspberries or any frozen berries for a little fiber, especially if you're suffering from any digestive issues. The yogurt contains probiotics to help aid in digestion.

Afternoon/Supper

Zinger Warming Soup (page 168) is my absolute favorite soup for a sick day. It's a great inflammation-fighting soup with turmeric and warming spices, it tastes amazing, and, being completely pureed, it is easy on digestion.

Turmeric Lemon Broth with Corona Beans (page 158) is a simple broth-based soup with potent herbs and spices and a little protein and fiber from the beans.

Black Rice Risotto with Mushrooms (page 217) is a warming, cozy, and satisfying risotto that is great for making leftovers and gives your body a warm, comforting meal that you may be craving.

The garlic in Turmeric and Garlic Root Mash (page 221) contains antimicrobial, antibacterial properties, and warming turmeric is an anti-inflammatory. This root veggie mash is bland enough to be easy on your tummy.

Dessert

Chocolate Fudge Paletas (page 259), made with natural sugars and fruit, provide a nice cooling effect if you need a little something soothing.

Bedtime

Turmeric Milk (page 69) and the Mushroom Tonic (page 76) contain antioxidants and anti-inflammatory compounds; they taste delicious; and they can be made warm/hot, which adds an extra oomph of comfort, or enjoyed chilled to soothe a throat. Turmeric—my favorite potent spice in my pantry—is found in both of these tonics.

NUTRIENTS A–Z

I often describe ingredients in my recipes as being nutrient dense or containing this vitamin or that mineral. Although it's great to know what food is rich in what nutrient, it's important to know why those vitamins and minerals are so important to your health. Here I've created a summary of vitamins and minerals, their role in the human body, amounts needed (which is a guideline based on the recommended daily allowances for adults), and the best food sources.

TERMS TO KNOW

DRIs: Dietary reference intakes are nutrient reference values developed by the Institute of Medicine of the National Academies. They serve as a guide for good nutrition and provide the scientific basis for the development of food guidelines in both the United States and Canada. DRI is the general term for a set of reference values used to plan and assess nutrient intakes of healthy people. These values, which vary by age and gender, include the following:

RDAs: Recommended dietary allowances represent the daily dietary intake of each vitamin and mineral[a] a person needs in order to maintain health and avoid nutritional deficiencies. RDAs are categorized to fit age and gender.

AI: For those vitamins for which an RDA has not yet been set (usually owing to lack of scientific data), the adequate intake level[b] is used in its place.

UL: Tolerable upper intake level[c] is the maximum amount of daily vitamin or mineral dosage that is likely to be safe for the "average" person, since each of our bodies is vastly different. To avoid toxicity, stay under the UL radar, especially when using supplements.

Measurements: Vitamins or minerals that are needed in larger doses are expressed in units of milligrams (mg). Trace minerals and vitamins are expressed in micrograms (mcg); 1 mg = 1,000 mcg.

VITAMINS (FAT SOLUBLE)

Vitamin A (retinoic acid, retinol, retinal): supports overall eye health, helps rebuild bone, regulates cell growth and division, decreases risk of certain cancers, keeps immune system and blood vessels healthy
Food sources: Provitamin A (most commonly beta-carotene): kale, eggs, sweet potatoes, carrots, pumpkins, cantaloupes, mangoes, butternut squash, vegetables in general. Preformed vitamin A: animal proteins such as meat, poultry, fish, and dairy

Vitamin D: maintains bone health and normal blood levels of calcium; strengthens bones/teeth; supports metabolism, nervous system function, and immune system function

Food sources: vitamin D–fortified foods/ milks, canned salmon, egg yolks, mushrooms grown in UV light (nonfood source: sunlight)

Vitamin E: protects lipids from damage, fights free radicals, maintains cell membrane integrity, protects vitamin A and fatty acids from oxidation
Food sources: plant oils, avocados, olive oil, nuts, seeds, egg yolks, whole grains, dark leafy greens

Vitamin K: aids in blood clotting
Food sources: Swiss chard, kale, other dark leafy greens, vegetables in general

VITAMINS (WATER SOLUBLE)

Vitamin B_1 (thiamine): helps energy metabolism with carbohydrates, promotes appetite control and normal digestion, maintains energy metabolism, supports nervous system function
Food sources: whole grains, quinoa, millet, legumes, beans, nuts, seeds, vegetables

Vitamin B_2 (riboflavin): helps the body convert energy from the food we eat; promotes healthy skin, hair, nails, muscle, and brain tissue; important part of maintaining normal vision
Food sources: wide variety of vegetables, whole grains, legumes

Vitamin B$_3$ (niacin, nicotinic acid, niacin amide): helps in energy production and metabolism; supports healthy skin, hair, and nails; promotes nervous system and digestive health function
Food sources: nuts, seeds, proteins, nutritional yeast, whole grains

Vitamin B$_5$ (pantothenic acid): supports metabolism
Food sources: wide variety of foods including vegetables, fruits, whole grains, beans, nuts, seeds

Vitamin B$_6$ (pyridoxine, pyridoxal): helps the body utilize and make nonessential amino acids, plays important role in protein metabolism
Food sources: green leafy vegetables, whole grains, legumes, fish, fruits

Vitamin B$_7$ (biotin): promotes healthy hair, skin, nails, cell growth, and general energy; also part of energy metabolism, fat synthesis, amino acid metabolism, and glycogen synthesis
Food sources: legumes, nuts, seeds, dark leafy greens, eggs, salmon, whole grains

Vitamin B$_{12}$ (cobalamin): allows the body to create new cells, maintains normal nervous system function (deficiencies of vitamin B$_{12}$ are common among plant-based diets)

Food sources: prevalent in animal proteins; fortified food products such as nutritional yeast, milk

Vitamin C (ascorbic acid): supports collagen production and formation; strengthens skin, blood vessels, and immune function; provides matrix for bone growth; fights free radicals; is an antioxidant; improves the absorption of iron (especially from nonheme sources)
Food sources: red bell peppers, citrus, dark leafy greens, vegetables generally, and fruits

Folic acid (folate, folacin): promotes blood cell formation and protein metabolism, prevents neural tube defects in infants, aids in energy and new cell synthesis
Food sources: most fortified U.S. foods, whole grains, vegetables, fruits, beans

MINERALS

Boron: supports bone health and prevention of osteoporosis
Food sources: fruits, leafy green vegetables

Calcium: promotes bone and teeth formation, supports normal muscle contraction (including skeletal/heart muscle tissues)
Food sources: fortified nondairy milk products, dark leafy greens, tahini, sesame seeds, tofu, broccoli, chard greens, legumes

Chloride: helps the body maintain normal balance of fluids and proper acid/base balance, essential for digestion
Food sources: salt

Chromium: releases energy from glucose, regulates insulin
Food sources: broccoli, whole grains, vegetables

Copper: supports healthy bones, muscles, blood vessels, iron absorption, immune function, energy metabolism, creation of blood cells
Food sources: nuts, seeds, legumes, beans, whole grains

Fluoride: involved in bone and teeth formation
Food sources: public water supplies, tea

Iodine: promotes thyroid and metabolism function; regulates thyroid hormones, tissue growth, and cell activity
Food sources: iodized salt, sea vegetables, seafood, vegetables

Iron: makes oxygen available to our muscles for contraction (including heart); vital for energy and overall health of collagen, neurotransmitters, and hormones (iron is a common deficiency)

Food sources: nonheme (plant-based sources) and heme (animal-based sources), including animal proteins, beans, legumes, nuts, seeds, dried fruit, eggs

Magnesium: promotes bone health, normal muscle contraction, transmission of nerve impulses; builds protein and energy; works with calcium; supports cell signaling; blood pressure regulation
Food sources: oats, nuts, seeds, bananas, avocados, dark leafy greens, molasses

Manganese: supports energy, bone development, wound healing, carbohydrate metabolism, and cholesterol
Food sources: nuts, seeds, wide variety of vegetables, fruits, whole grains

Molybdenum: fortifies enzymatic systems and processes
Food sources: legumes, beans, nuts, seeds, wide variety of foods

Phosphorus: promotes and maintains bone and teeth building; helps convert food we eat into energy, shuttling nutrients to our organs and body as needed
Food sources: dairy, abundant in vegetables, legumes

Potassium: balances the body's fluids; aids in smooth muscle contraction (heart), transmission of nervous system signals, and muscle function

Food sources: avocados, bananas, tomatoes, potatoes, artichokes, plums, vegetables

Selenium: supports thyroid health, protects from free-radical damage

Food sources: Brazil nuts, whole grains, nuts, seeds, salmon

Sulfur: helps shape and stabilize protein structures; promotes hair, skin, and nail health

Food sources: cruciferous vegetables and protein-rich foods, nuts, seeds, legumes

Zinc: plays role in skin health, serves as building block for proteins and cells, frees vitamin A from the liver, aids in immune function support and wound healing, needed for taste and smell

Food sources: pumpkin seeds, sesame seeds, oysters, animal proteins, cashews

Resources: Office of Dietary Supplements, Consumer Labs, Food and Nutrition Board, Institute of Medicine, National Academies

a. http://www.iom.edu/Activities/Nutrition/SummaryDRIs/~/media/Files/Activity%20Files/Nutrition/DRIs/5_Summary%20Table%20Tables%201-4.pdf

b. http://www.webmd.com/vitamins-and-supplements/lifestyle-guide-11/vitamins-minerals-how-much-should-you-take

c. http://www.umm.edu/patiented/articles/what_vitamins_000039_1.htm

ACKNOWLEDGMENTS

Working on this cookbook was a joy—from conception to the testing of hundreds of recipes to make sure they were both healthy and delicious!

Each time I created a new recipe, I thought of you. I thought of how I could make healthy eating simple, delicious, and truly nourishing utilizing whole foods that are vital to your health. You're the reason why I created the Nutrition Stripped blog in the first place, and to create this book for you was a joy. To the Nutrition Stripped community: I love you guys! If it weren't for you making my recipes with your friends and family, providing feedback, sharing on social media, and bringing the Nutrition Stripped philosophy into your own lifestyle, I wouldn't have made a cookbook. Truly, you are the core of Nutrition Stripped and I'm eternally grateful for your support.

To each friend, family member, and reader, for recipe testing. Your feedback was invaluable and helped the dishes in this book to be as delicious as they possibly could be.

To my clients, you continue to inspire me each day with your determination and motivation to reach your health and wellness goals to feel your best; you keep my own well-being in check.

To the Nutrition Stripped team, including my assistant, photographers, designers, tech team, and interns in San Francisco during the cookbook shoot, for all your hard work, passion, and support to bring this cookbook to life; I'm so thankful for you and couldn't do it alone. Go Team!

To the Nashville community, you all are beautiful, encouraging, and creative spirits who keep me on my toes and challenge me to be a better person and leader in my field. For that, I thank you for all the good vibes.

To my literary agent, Sharon, for being one of the first cheerleaders for the development of this book and for finding the right publishing team to execute it. To my editor, Cara Bedick, for your refining skills and attention to detail that made this book more enjoyable to read; and to the amazing publishing team who brought the recipes to life within every page, especially Ashley Tucker, Rachel Meyers, Katherine Turro, and Anwesha Basu.

Last, a huge thank-you to the friends and family who have supported me throughout this entire process. Even when Mom told me, "This recipe is kinda weird, but I like it," it encouraged a more flexible approach. Thank you for believing in me wholeheartedly in building Nutrition Stripped to what it is today on this crazy beautiful journey with all its ups and downs. For continuing to challenge me to expand Nutrition Stripped into something I've always dreamed of, a community and cause bigger than me. I thank you and love each of you with all my heart. I truly wouldn't be here writing this today if it weren't for you. I love you, I love you, I love you!

FAVORITE INGREDIENTS AND PRODUCTS

Writing and being involved with the health and wellness industry has opened tremendous doors and opportunities for me to try some of the most amazing, well-thought-out, healthful-living, and whole-food products I never dreamed of! I love being able to support small businesses and helping spread the word about products that I truly enjoy using myself. Here is a list of brands and products I've genuinely fallen in love with over the years and I hope you'll try them when you stumble upon them.

FOOD

GRAINS
Bob's Red Mill

Lotus Foods

Shiloh Farms

NUTS AND SEEDS
Nuts.com

Artisana

Rawmio nut butters

Windy City Organics nut butters

SPECIALTY
Panatea matcha green tea

Yogi tea

Traditional Medicinals teas

Organic Gemini tigernuts

Moon Juice juices

Fire cider

Maine Coast Sea Vegetables (for seaweeds and seaweed flakes)

Eden Foods

Coconut Secret (for coconut nectar, vinegar, flour, etc.)

Miso Master

Penzeys Spices

Frontier Natural Products Co-op spices and herbs

Flower Power Herbs and Roots (for roses, lavender, etc.)

Bragg raw apple cider vinegar and oils

Jarrow Formulas (probiotics)

Belle+Bella yogurt starters

SNACKS
Just Hemp hemp seeds

Purely Elizabeth snacks

Unreal snacks and chocolate

Simply 7 snacks

Kite Hill vegan cheese

One Degree Organics cereal

Nourish Snacks

Pipsnacks popcorn

Apotheker's chocolate and marshmallows

JJ's Cocomels

KIND Healthy Snacks

CONDIMENTS

Mike's Hot Honey

Hummus Chick Hummus

Mina Harissa

NUTRIENT-DENSE POWDERS AND BOOSTERS

Philosophie superfood powders

Bare Blends berry and green powders

Nutiva Naturals superfoods

Aloha greens powder

Organic Bursts superfood powders

Sambazon açaí

Pitaya dragon fruit

Moon Juice powdered mushrooms

Sun Potion mushroom powders

PROTEIN POWDERS

Bare Blends protein and green/berry powder

Sunwarrior

Vega Sport

Sprout Living Epic Protein

MISCELLANEOUS

Rainbow Light Advanced Enzyme System

FITNESS APPAREL

Lululemon

Nike

Lucy Activewear

Nutrition Stripped T-shirts!

BOOKS

Crazy Sexy Diet
by Kris Carr

Food Matters
by Mark Bittman

Food Politics
by Marion Nestle

Food Rules
by Michael Pollan

In Defense of Food
by Michael Pollan

Mindful Eating
by Brian Wansink

Savor: Mindful Eating, Mindful Life
by Thich Naht Hanh

Omnivores Dilemma
by Michael Pollan

What to Eat
by Marion Nestle

What to Eat: The Ten Things You Really Need to Know to Eat Well and Be Healthy by Luise Light

World's Healthiest Foods
by George Mateljin

MEDITATION

Headspace (meditation app)

Gabrielle Bernstein guided meditations

Thich Naht Han books

Eckhart Tolle, the Power of Now series

UNIVERSAL CONVERSION CHART

OVEN TEMPERATURE EQUIVALENTS

250°F = 120°C   400°F = 200°C

275°F = 135°C   425°F = 220°C

300°F = 150°C   450°F = 230°C

325°F = 160°C   475°F = 240°C

350°F = 180°C   500°F = 260°C

375°F = 190°C

MEASUREMENT EQUIVALENTS

Measurements should always be level unless directed otherwise.

⅛ teaspoon = 0.5 mL

¼ teaspoon = 1 mL

½ teaspoon = 2 mL

1 teaspoon = 5 mL

1 tablespoon = 3 teaspoons = ½ fluid ounce = 15 mL

2 tablespoons = ⅛ cup = 1 fluid ounce = 30 mL

4 tablespoons = ¼ cup = 2 fluid ounces = 60 mL

5⅓ tablespoons = ⅓ cup = 3 fluid ounces = 80 mL

8 tablespoons = ½ cup = 4 fluid ounces = 120 mL

10⅔ tablespoons = ⅔ cup = 5 fluid ounces = 160 mL

12 tablespoons = ¾ cup = 6 fluid ounces = 180 mL

16 tablespoons = 1 cup = 8 fluid ounces = 240 mL

INDEX

Note: Page numbers in *italics* refer to illustrations.

ABOUT THE AUTHOR

McKel Hill, MS, RDN, is a Registered Dietitian Nutritionist and founder of Nutrition Stripped. Nutrition Stripped is a healthful living website dedicated to optimizing well-being through recipes, nutrition advice, and fitness, which recently launched the Society—a healthy meal planning and wellness membership. McKel is a nutrition expert and contributor at Cameron Diaz's blog, The Body Book, and her work has been featured on FoodNetwork.com and in *Glamour, Vogue, Bon Appétit, Women's Health Magazine, Real Simple, Eating Well, SHAPE, Town & Country, Thrive,* and many other publications. McKel is one of a new breed of dietitian nutritionists who are leading the tribe for wellness.